SUPER
GIRLS
★★★ AND ★★★
HALOS

"What do you get when you cross Wonder Woman and Hermione Granger with St. Katharine Drexel and St. Clare of Assisi? You'll have to read this unique book to find out! Maria Morera Johnson's love of films is eclipsed only by her love of books. In her latest offering, *Super Girls and Halos*, she introduces a series of gutsy women who help us explore what is good in our own souls. Even though I'm not the science-fiction geek or literature professor that Johnson is, I loved her unexpected and eclectic pairings of intriguing heroines of the screen and the page alongside inspiring saints of the Church. This PG-rated mingling of fiction, films, and faith stories is a fab follow up to *My Badass Book of Saints*! It's serious fun mixed with the joy of faith!"

Pat Gohn
Author of *Blessed, Beautiful, and Bodacious*

"Superheroes and saints prove to be an irresistible combination. Maria Johnson has managed to expertly tell the stories of both with an eye toward the inner desires God has given each of us. This is the very best kind of catechesis and sure to be your favorite read of the year!"

Sarah Reinhard
Catholic author, writer, and managing editor of *Today's Catholic Teacher*

"With wit and wisdom, Maria Morera Johnson pairs the excitement and adventure of fictional heroines with the integrity and tenacity of true heroines who walked this earth. This clever combination packs a punch, providing us with a powerful lesson on righteousness and inspiring us to live with the confidence needed to become virtuous heroines and heroic saints. A must-read for anyone looking to tap into her supernatural, God-given powers!"

Kelly Wahlquist
Founder of WINE: Women In the New Evangelization
and editor of *Walk in Her Sandals*

"Maria Morera Johnson has put together a collection of real and fictional heroines who deliver real kicks (and gentle taps) of correction to the notion that a colorful woman may lack moral wisdom or that a gentle woman is deficient in spiritual and social strength. Try telling that to St. Katharine Drexel, Dana Scully, or Wonder Woman! These sisters are full of the right stuff, and Johnson serves up their virtues with a *pow!* and a prayer."

Elizabeth Scalia
US editor of *Aleteia* and author of *Strange Gods*

SUPER GIRLS

★★★ AND ★★★

HALOS

MY COMPANIONS ON THE QUEST FOR TRUTH, JUSTICE, AND HEROIC VIRTUE

MARIA MORERA JOHNSON

AVE MARIA PRESS AVE Notre Dame, Indiana

Founded in 1865, Ave Maria Press is a ministry of the United States Province of Holy Cross.

www.avemariapress.com

Paperback: ISBN-13 978-1-59471-755-0

E-book: ISBN-13 978-1-59471-756-7

Cover and text design by Katherine J. Ross.

Printed and bound in the United States of America.

Library of Congress Cataloging-in-Publication Data is available.

CONTENTS

INTRODUCTION

HEROINES, HEROIC VIRTUE, AND THE QUEST FOR GOOD

No capes!

—Edna Mode, *The Incredibles*

Edna Mode, the feisty tailor to the superheroes from the animated film *The Incredibles,* refuses to make any super-hero costumes with capes. She's not interested in the flashy appearance or the popular opinion of what makes a great costume. Edna sizes up Mr. Incredible's ideas for his new look and goes for the jugular: "No capes!"

Sartorial advice aside, Edna makes a great point: capes get in the way of performance. Her delivery is hilarious, punctuated by example after example of superheroes experiencing tragic consequences while wearing capes. The heroes are caught up in looking the part of hero instead of focusing on the practical reality. They have a job to do, and Edna wants to help by providing the best possible protection. Capes contribute nothing. In fact, capes are detrimental.

Edna doesn't just discourage poor costume choice for her clients; she also wants them to think outside the box. Edna encourages them to focus on their skills, *their gifts,* and *use* them.

That advice rings true for all of us. We should discard any "capes" that distract us from who we are, whether that cape is a social construct or our own voices in our heads that limit and discourage us from doing the very best we can do. These capes distract us from what is good, true, and beautiful.

THE HERO'S MISSION

Edna Mode works with superheroes, men and women who fight against crime and the evil threatening society. This theme of crime-fighting and, on a larger scale, the drive for good to triumph over evil, appears over and over again in popular stories, whether traditional literary series such as the Harry Potter saga and The Hunger Games or less classical modes of storytelling such as comic books and graphic novels. These adventures lend themselves to television and film because of the epic nature of the stories. Add the visual appeal of modern special effects, and the fantastical seems real. We can envision ourselves in the roles we see on the screen and respond to these courageous characters with admiration and appreciation for the fortitude or integrity they exhibit. Characters such as Katniss Everdeen and Wonder Woman often resonate with us because we admire their virtues. We might live vicariously through their fictional adventures, but can emulate their traits, such as courage or justice, in our daily lives.

REAL-LIFE HEROES

When I was six years old, my father sat me down in front of our little black-and-white television set to watch Neil Armstrong walk on the moon. I had no real understanding of what was going on, but I could feel the excitement in my father's voice, and the sense of wonder that something very special was happening. My mother sat in a corner of the living room with my baby brother in her arms, and my father—well, he was all over the place, standing, sitting, talking, and directing me to place my chubby little hand *just so* on the television screen.

Pop took a picture of my hand against the bright glare of the television broadcasting the moonwalk. He said I touched the future.

The impression of that moment started a lifelong love of space and all the science fiction associated with it. You'd think my father's obsession with the NASA space program would lead me down a path to the sciences. It did, in a way, but it also opened up my imagination, which developed an interest in storytelling. I wanted to know what those men were doing while bouncing around the lunar surface in their spacesuits, and I imagined them performing great exploits. I tried so hard to see UFOs in the sky, and I wasn't afraid of being abducted by aliens. (Well, except that one time when I was eleven and the Goodyear blimp came out from behind some cloud cover. I thought I really was witnessing an extra-terrestrial invasion!)

The moment impressed me in another way, too. My dad, who was *my* hero, had heroes of his own. It was a small lesson with a big impact: grown-ups had heroes who were other grown-ups. It was a funny idea to a six-year-old, but today, grown-up me has lots of grown-up heroes. I call them saints. But first, I followed my dad's early lead and looked to space for heroes and role models.

MY FIRST HERO:
LT. UHURA

My love of space drew me to science fiction stories. I'd sit on my father's lap while he watched *Star Trek* on Sunday nights. I was too young to understand the show during its original run in the 1960s, but reruns in the '70s captivated me and fueled my growing imagination. I couldn't get enough of those stories. I was still a kid, and Lt. Uhura from *Star Trek* was my hero. I have a scar in my ear canal from wearing a metal spring I swiped from my little brother's crib. It looked like the communication device Uhura wore in her ear, so it was great for pretending.

There were several women on *Star Trek* besides Lieutenant Uhura, but she was definitely the coolest. Uhura was a communications officer. I didn't know what that was, but even then the rumblings from my friends' older sisters told me that Lt. Uhura was a wise choice for a role model. Feminism had gained a stronghold in the high school girls' world, and they were vocal about anything that might cast women, especially some of the women we saw on television, as tired old clichés of womanhood. I looked to these high school–age older sisters of friends as authorities on all things feminine.

These young feminists focused on the roles the women played: a female yeoman attracted to Capt. Kirk and a female nurse who assisted a male doctor. The big sisters were disappointed in the limitations of the jobs offered to women. Lt. Uhura, on the other hand, didn't seem tied down to any man, and her role was nontraditional. She was a woman on the bridge of a starship, and she held her own as an expert in her field.

FEMINISM OR FEMININE GENIUS?

As an undergraduate student of literature, I thought male and female characters could have interchangeable attributes. I rejected the view that a female character could bring to the role of hero something unique to her character that went beyond what I knew to be sexist and clichéd representations of their characters.

Then I discovered the feminine genius through St. John Paul II's *Letter to Women* and *Mulieris Dignitatum* (*On the Dignity and Vocation of Women*). St. John Paul II stresses that women have a unique gift in being life-bearers, that because we can bring life into the world through this gift of our female biology, we also have a special vocation to be caretakers of God's human creation. We are called, because we are women, to care for others.

As women we can, as Pope Benedict XVI says, "make a sincere gift of ourselves to others."[1] This is an important aspect of the feminine genius, openness to all life and the desire to care for it with tenderness and hope.

God not only created us out of love, but he also created us for love. As women, we express that love in unique ways. Pat Gohn, author of *Blessed, Beautiful, and Bodacious: Celebrating the Gift of Catholic Womanhood*, identifies the special ways we live out our feminine genius: "Women are uniquely endowed with gifts of receptivity, generosity, sensitivity, and maternity. When we trust these things, we become beautiful from the inside out. We live the lives we are born to live, becoming the best women we can be."[2]

In receptivity, a woman sees and accepts the value of love and relationship everywhere around her. Sensitivity allows her to see beyond herself to the needs of others. Thus, she is also generous—not just to the needs of one person but to society. She sees the whole in addition to the immediacy of the one. Finally, maternity uniquely equips her not only for building family through her physical capabilities but also for building family and community outside herself.

As a lover of literature, I find that the most compelling, realistic characters are those that remain true to their natures. Female characters that are represented with plausible and believable attributes, both positive and negative, are the characters that I most connect with and that resonate with me.

This feminine genius is not suppressed in the modern female heroine. We see it in modern female characters, specifically heroines of the science fiction and fantasy that dominate the big and small screens, especially literary texts that are brought to life in film. When the writers take pains to present the characters in realistic ways, I buy into the characters' authenticity. I don't just want to live vicariously as they live; I want to adopt their virtues.

An appreciation for the larger-than-life pursuits of these fictional women gives us a taste of what real virtue can be. These characters bring into focus a certain reality about life when see ourselves in them. Aspects of the feminine genius complement the heroism exhibited by the characters in this book. However, we see the full strength of this genius, this mission of womanhood, in the lives of the saints.

HEROINES

I like my movies to have big explosions and happy endings. I can get by without the explosions, but I want good to triumph over evil. Every time, please.

Comic book heroes and their exploits are all over the movies today. It used to be nerdy to collect comics, and serious conversations about the characters were unheard of when I was younger. The first comic book heroes were pretty one-dimensional, and there wasn't much to discuss. We knew who the good guys were and what their values were, and we knew who the bad guys were and watched their evil ways.

They'd fight. The bad guy would get a good hold on the good guy and things would look bleak for a moment. Then our hero would find some last bit of strength, drawn perhaps deeply from within his soul, and rally back until the bad guy was defeated. Add an explosion. *Bam! Pow!* The girl gets rescued. They live happily ever after. At least until the next bad guy messes up the status quo again.

Today's superhero has evolved. No longer a one-dimensional character, the modern superhero tends to be flawed. Although most of these fictional heroes are men, the second half of the twentieth century saw an increase in female superheroes, and the twenty-first century has exploded with compelling female action characters. These fictional women, these heroines, have bridged the genres beyond the comics into science fiction, fantasy, and adventure. We still enjoy Wonder Woman from the comics, but we have other larger-than-life characters such as Katniss Everdeen from *The Hunger Games* and Rey from *Star Wars: The Force Awakens*.

THE VIRTUOUS HERO

Most of us can list the attributes of our favorite heroes or heroines. We might even casually say it's a list of their virtues. The traits can be varied: I might describe a character as honest, courageous, and stalwart while someone else might describe the same character as brave, daring, and courteous. Most lists describe good qualities of the person.

We'd never describe a villain as virtuous, nor would we call his attributes virtues. That's because in our everyday use of the word, we can usually agree that we're talking about the things that make up someone's character as being morally good.

To discuss virtue in the context of the Catholic faith, we turn to the *Catechism of the Catholic Church* for a definition: "A virtue is a habitual and firm disposition to do the good. It allows the person not only to perform good acts, but to give the best of himself" (*CCC*, 1803).

With this definition in mind, we can take any of those positive attributes discussed above and call them human virtues. These are habits that help make us morally good. We call them human virtues because it is up to us to practice them in order to achieve the habit. It's a causal thing—to become honest, for example, I must endeavor to tell the truth always; by telling the truth always, I will become honest.

These human virtues, which are numerous, can be grouped, or classified, under four areas, called the cardinal virtues. They are justice, prudence, fortitude, and temperance. In characters such as Wonder Woman from DC Comics, we see the pursuit of justice; prudence is at work in Agent Dana Scully from *The X-Files*, and in Hermione Granger from Harry Potter, we see fortitude in conviction. Katniss Everdeen from *The Hunger Games* shows temperance and self-control in a vicious setting outside of her control.

Characters such as these can inspire us to grow in virtue. However, we cannot attain these virtues without God's saving grace. As we move from the heroines' stories to the lives of saints, we see how the cardinal virtues, strengthened by God's grace, led these women to holiness. We learn through these saints that we grow in virtue by practicing the tenets of our faith, too. Frequent reception of the sacraments, unwavering trust in the Lord, prayer—all of these things, in cooperation with God's grace, bring us closer to God.

Through our baptism, we also receive God's gift of the theological virtues: faith, hope, and charity. These gifts help us perfect our cardinal virtues—justice, prudence, fortitude, and temperance—something we can't do on our own. We must work with God, and God works in us. Unlike the heroines who depend only upon themselves and the development of their human virtues, the saints, cooperating with God's plan, receive the gifts of the Holy Spirit to help them grow in holiness. They accept God's will in their lives, regardless of the sacrifice or tedium. This can be called heroic virtue.

How much greater would our experience be if we looked to real-life heroines, the canonized saints, who lived extraordinary lives of virtues? Their stories, when held up to us, are not mirrored distortions but paths to holiness. We can learn to cultivate their virtues—the cardinal virtues of prudence, justice, fortitude, and temperance and the theological virtues of faith, hope, and charity—that certainly lead us to the good but ultimately will lead us to the one God.

WE NEED HEROES.
WE NEED HEROINES.

Many of these fictional heroes rise to the level of hero because circumstances demand it. They find themselves in situations that require action, extraordinary action that only they can perform because of their unique skills.

Few of us live dramatic lives of extraordinary heroics that involve saving the world, but I think all of us are called to lives of extraordinary virtue—lives that present challenges only we can overcome because of the gifts we have, gifts from God that are meant to be used and celebrated.

The fictional women in this book experience the heroic journey. They respond to the challenges using their unique set of skills, be it tactical savvy, diplomatic aplomb, or intellectual analysis. While their circumstances differ and their characters feature different traits, they share a common strength in their feminine sensibilities. The female hero—the heroine—embraces her feminine traits and succeeds because of doing so.

The real-life heroine protects, embraces, encourages, and listens with sensitivity. The heroine seeks the good, the true, and the beautiful in people and the world. In pursuing these ideals, the heroine is ultimately pursuing God, who is goodness, truth, and beauty. The heroine brings love into her relationships, and in doing so, opens up greater possibilities for all the persons she encounters.

The super girls and halos in this book truly are companions on the quest for heroic virtue. I explore my favorite heroines of science fiction, fantasy, and comics as they seek the good. "Anyone who sets off on the path of doing good to others is already drawing near to God, is already sustained by his help, for it is characteristic of the divine light to brighten our eyes whenever we walk toward the fullness of love."[3] I share what makes these characters extraordinary and what makes them exciting role models. Their search for the good contains what Bishop Robert Barron calls "*semina verbi* (seeds of the word)."[4] These characters exhibit qualities that are close to the Gospel and become a good starting point for a conversation about refining the cardinal virtues. As part of that conversation, I introduce the reader to real-life women, saints who have lived lives of heroic virtue—not filled with fictional powers but flesh and blood women receptive to the almighty power of God.

Edna would be pleased to know there isn't a cape in the bunch.

PART I

★

SEEKING
JUSTICE

When I think of justice, images of a judge pounding a gavel and yelling "Order in the court!" come to mind. Modern concerns about laws and due process—whether for status, rights, or obligations—predispose us to think of justice in legalistic terms. We might also think of iconic Lady Justice, blindfolded and holding a balance and a sword, to signify objectivity, reason, and punishment.

These images may be representative of society's expectations, but justice as a cardinal virtue carries a different definition, along with an exhortation to act.

The *Catholic Encyclopedia* says it is a "habit which perfects the will and inclines it to render to each and to all what belongs to them."[1] That's fair.

Fairness is part of it, but it's a little more complex—the *Catechism of the Catholic Church* states it a little more broadly: "*Justice* is the moral virtue that consists in the constant and firm will to give their due to God and neighbor. Justice toward God is called the 'virtue of religion.' Justice toward men disposes one to respect the rights of each and to establish in human relationships the harmony that promotes equity with regard to persons and to the common good" (*CCC*, 1807).

It's about being good to our neighbors, but it's also about giving God his due—we ought to do more than believe in God; we need to worship him.

The women in this section each manifest this virtue differently in their lives. Wonder Woman seeks the kind of justice we're most familiar with—justice applied to society so it runs smoothly, good guys doing good things, and bad guys put away where they won't cause harm. In Rey we see how pursuing peace promotes justice in a galaxy committed to seeking the common good. The saints offer us models of holy virtue. St. Katharine Drexel recognizes that despite a society built upon the common good, there are marginalized peoples everywhere that deserve, in fact are due, social justice. St. Clare's witness as a true believer shows us how right and just it is to serve and worship God.

CRUSADERS OF JUSTICE AND LEARNING

WONDER WOMAN AND ST. KATHARINE DREXEL

Please take my hand. I give it to you as a gesture of friendship and love, and of faith freely given.

—Wonder Woman, *Wonder Woman #167*

I can't decide whether I want Wonder Woman's bracelets or her lasso of truth as my go-to accessory. She is prepared to kick ass with both in the 2017 release of *Wonder Woman*. I've been waiting a long time for a great action film featuring this heroine and so have a lot of women. While superheroines appear in recent blockbusters, characters such as Black Widow and Storm play supporting roles in ensembles. It's exciting to see a superheroine as the protagonist of the film.

I don't even mind the modern rendition that has altered Wonder Woman's origin story. In fact, I embrace it whole-heartedly. Comic book heroes have long been subjected to the *retcon*, short for retroactive continuity, to add, enhance, and sometimes change information in the character's canon in order to justify new storylines. Superheroes have been around for decades, some for almost a hundred years. Writers change, times change, and it all makes sense that the occasional deviation from the storyline might need to be explained.

Sometimes the retcon is artfully done and enriches the story, and other times it is gratuitous and the result of lazy writing. Wonder Woman has seen both. She debuted in December 1941, placed in World War II–storylines and working as a US Army in her secret identity as Diana Prince. Since then, Wonder Woman has been through at least four iterations in the comics and several more in television live-action and animation series. All these place her in different settings with different personality traits to better play into the social norms of the times. Diana has gone from warrior princess to ambassador and back again. She even lost her superpowers for a brief time and opened a mod boutique. *Yuck.* Yet I love that in spite of these changes her basic human dignity and desire to do good in the world remains. Wonder Woman is, and always has been, an advocate of justice.

The trend to reboot comic book characters' origin stories, that is, completely change their histories in order to better fit new social expectations or take the stories in new directions and interpretations, has affected Wonder Woman too. While the new Wonder Woman, daughter of Zeus, jumps into the scene as a formidable force in the world, the original Wonder Woman, crafted from clay, still intrigues me. While I know that an updated version of Wonder Woman likely appeals to modern sensibilities, her origin story attracted my curiosity. I wondered how she changed over the years and what contributed to the traits we see on the big screen today. After all, I'm not the same woman I was thirty years ago or even ten years ago. To better understand her impact today, I needed to know her beginnings.

FEMINIST ICON? NOT SO MUCH

I read my share of comic books when I was a girl, and I watched the Saturday-morning and after-school animated series that were developed as a response to the comics' popularity. I knew the Wonder Woman from the 1960s and 1970s—a Wonder Woman who fought alongside Batman and Superman and worked as Diana for the United Nations. I didn't see her as a feminist icon but rather as just another superhero.

Those stories definitely encouraged my interest in science fiction and in more complex stories as I got older. By the time I was in college and majoring in English, I was drawn to reading materials that weren't mainstream. I enrolled in many special topics courses in science fiction, genre studies, and one of my favorites at the time, a women-in-literature course. Ever pushing the envelope, I chose to do my research on comic book heroines and focused on Wonder Woman. She proved to be a disappointment. I found she was written in a cheeky style that was sometimes too preachy and other times too meek for me to believe she was a superhero. I dismissed her for decades.

Years later, my interest in her was piqued when I heard that producer Joss Whedon was working on a Wonder Woman feature film. Whedon had written and produced the popular series *Buffy the Vampire Slayer* as well as *Firefly*, one of my favorite sci-fi television series. His characters in both series are complex and strong, so I was excited to see his vision for Wonder Woman. The Wonder Woman project was ultimately scrapped, but through the intriguing possibility of this project I rediscovered Wonder Woman.

This time, I had a different angle for appreciating Wonder Woman. Not only had I matured, I also had the confidence that comes from success in my vocations. I was happily married, launching my kids to college, and enjoying a renewal in my career. That seed of curiosity, and if I may use the word, my *reconciliation* with my earlier views of Wonder Woman, left me wanting to read more about this heroine. I thought Wonder Woman had the potential to be a great role model for the twenty-first century: she embodied the gifts of womanhood in a way that contrasted with many discussions of gender in the public forum.

Wonder Woman's creator, psychologist William Moulton Marston, wanted a heroine "who would triumph not with fists or firepower but with love."[1] This concept for the character intrigued me, although I admit it took me many years to not only accept this but also understand it in a heroine. Superman didn't have to love anyone. Respect, yes. Admire, maybe. But love? I hadn't realized the importance of love in a superhero when I was a young woman. I got it now that my maturity included a growing understanding of my faith.

The more I encountered St. John Paul II's writings about the feminine genius and the special gifts of women, the more I looked with a discerning eye at the kinds of role models I had been selecting in the past. As a young woman, I had turned to mainstream characters in popular culture for cues about my feminine identity. These include some of the fictional characters I discuss here. I still like these heroines. There's much to admire in their virtues, but now I see that they fulfill only a piece of what I desire in a role model. These heroines, with Wonder Woman at the forefront, lead with a profound sense of their mission to protect the weak and vulnerable in society. I became drawn to saints who exhibited the same traits but also desired to fulfill God's will in their lives. I had been putting my stock in fictional characters when I had the Communion of Saints for true inspiration.

FROM PSYCHOLOGY TO COMICS

Marston is perhaps best known as the creator of the technology behind the lie detector (knowing this, I think it's pretty funny that Wonder Woman uses a lasso of truth). His work was not in studying literature but in studying people. Much of his initial research focused on honesty in the workplace and the hypothesis that women tended to be more honest than men in workplace settings. His work was discredited for not following proper scientific protocols, but his anecdotal findings helped him begin to formulate the basic traits that would one day lead to the creation of Wonder Woman.

Max Gaines, publisher of the forerunner to today's DC Comics, hired Marston as a psychological consultant. From there, Marston started writing for Gaines and eventually suggested the creation of a female superhero. Marston took his inspiration for this superhero from the inroads made in women's suffrage and from America's emerging feminism movement. Marston executed this plan for a modern female hero by the end of 1941. It was this Wonder Woman that I read in my feminist undergraduate days, and it was also this preachy and meek Wonder Woman that made me sad. She was designed to be the new superwoman. Conceptually she was, but in execution, the writing and artwork lacked continuity with this vision.

Different illustrators, all men, drew Wonder Woman, so there were aesthetic differences in her appearance ranging from modest to sexy. Perhaps the intent wasn't to create a pinup girl, but Wonder Woman definitely shows more skin than the male superheroes. The writing, too, failed to live up to the potential for this groundbreaking character. Although she managed to extricate herself from dangerous situations, Diana was often portrayed as a damsel in distress. Marston might have envisioned a new kind of hero, but he and the other writers put Diana into situations where her leadership was not explored. The visionary Marston still acquiesced to societal expectations.

Nevertheless, Marston believed women would emerge as excellent leaders because they had uniquely feminine attributes that brought sensitivity and nurturing to the forefront of their interactions. In defending a superwoman to counter the parental complaints about violence in comic books, Marston said, "A male hero, at best, lacks the qualities of maternal love and tenderness which are as essential to a normal child as the breath of life."[2] He believed that women's relational skills complement the aggressive traits exhibited by male superheroes. Wonder Woman didn't just capture the bad guys and foil their plans; she spoke to them and appealed to the good in them. This difference was overt enough for me to come away with the feeling that she was too preachy when I first read her. In fact, Wonder Woman's maternal instinct was often the highlight of the storyline. In later readings though, I was surprised to find inklings of St. John Paul II's feminine genius in Wonder Woman!

As a young feminist first reading about Wonder Woman, I wanted to reject all the feminine trappings exhibited in the character. I wanted my heroes, male and female, to be interchangeable. I didn't want a heroine with intuition. I didn't want a heroine who spoke softly and listened. And I certainly didn't want a heroine in a skirt: that just added insult to injury. And yet, even in skirts, Wonder Woman commanded respect and was an influential addition to the superhero universe. If nothing else, the mere presence of a female character in the midst of this male-dominated genre made the statement that women had a place in this world, that in fact women *were* a part of this world. I owe much to that Wonder Woman, even if at first I didn't like the traditional roles she embraced. I was especially annoyed with her joining the Justice Society of America in 1942. This organization of superheroes gathered together to uphold American values such as justice. However, what should have been an opportunity to showcase Wonder Woman's skills as a peacemaker within the fictional organization failed. The writers made her the secretary of the Justice Society and wrote her out of the action.

Eventually, I accepted that Wonder Woman had certain feminine traits, such as sensitivity, and that she was created to demonstrate how love is a powerful motivator, especially in her sincere care and nursing of Steve Trevor, her love interest. What I rejected was the condescending way Wonder Woman was sometimes written. Most of Wonder Woman's adventures fit a generic story arc. During the early years, she was mostly fighting the enemies of the United States. She would often be captured and bound, and then she would escape and take down the bad guys. The stories were at once forgettable and patriotic. There were stories where she definitely saves the day and others where she is relegated to supporting character. In almost every instance, however, her purpose was the support of the common good.

Those early years had a kind of split personality for Diana, which depended on who was her writer at the time.

For example, throughout her early years, Steve Trevor tries to get her to give up these activities and marry him. Diana entertained the idea of marriage in some storylines but in others rejected it, citing that she would have to give up her life of adventure as she knew it. Not only did these vacillations leave a bad taste in my mouth, but I also wanted to hear Wonder Woman tell me I could have it all: a family and a career.

Even though I wanted to be a strong feminist, I didn't want to give up the other side—I wanted to get married and have a family, and I would happily have given up my career to do it. Wonder Woman and I were on the opposite side of the feminism chasm created by the public discourse, which sometimes implied women could, and should, pursue careers instead of families. Part of me wanted Wonder Woman to show me I could have both. I went on to have both: a family and a career. On good days, I had it all. On bad days, I was at work, pining for my family, or at home, thinking about the things I left undone at work. I wanted justice for everyone, all the things my family and students deserved, but I felt like the loser.

Wonder Woman, like me, struggled to find her place in a man's world. She wanted to work for what is good and right in the world. Justice was more than an ideal, it was an attainable end, and she fought the good fight to promote it.

However, despite her fight for justice, I don't believe that Wonder Woman encompasses a completely feminist ideal. She leaves her home to take Steve Trevor, an injured pilot, back to the United States. She has fallen in love with him and first nurses him to health before becoming his secretary. I'd say her introduction to the United States was self-serving in spite of her subsequent contribution to the pursuit of justice.

Some feminists might take issue with Wonder Woman's motivation to pursue a man. The phrase "a woman without a man is like a fish without a bicycle" became a kind of rallying call for feminists in the early 1970s, yet Gloria Steinem launched *Ms.* magazine in 1972 with Wonder Woman on the cover—the heroine whose *raison d'être* was Steve Trevor.

It seems to me that when it comes to Wonder Woman, we want it all. We want Wonder Woman to be strong, independent, and successful but also sensitive, nurturing, and feminine. As I, no longer a militant feminist, think about this today, I realize these seemingly contradictory desires might fit well with feminist ideals after all.

Surprisingly, they also fit well within the Catholic understanding of the new feminism. Wonder Woman drew strength from her feminine gifts. Marston's pitch to publisher Gaines hints at his personal feelings: "Look, if you had a female superhero, her powers could all be about love and truth and beauty, and you could also sell your comic books better to girls. And that would be really important and great because she could show girls that they could do anything."[3] Marston knew that a woman's nature was different from a man's. Not better, but different.

ENCOMPASSING
THE FEMININE GIFTS

William Marston's desire to create a superwoman introduced a new dynamic to the otherwise all-male heroes in the comic book genre. Nevertheless, Wonder Woman never became that superwoman. Her character's development was flawed almost from the beginning and was destined to fail because of sloppy continuity by writers who never understood Marston's vision or feminism. She changed according to the writers' interpretations of her, at one point actually becoming the direct opposite of what Marston had in mind: the post–World War II Wonder Woman was meek and submissive, but Marston's vision allowed for a character who was strong, a powerful leader who demonstrated a feminine side that enhances her leadership rather than limits it.

Marston's insistence that Wonder Woman have these feminine attributes runs counter to his peers' thoughts on feminism: "Feminists rejected the idea of women as reformers whose moral authority came from their differentness from men—women were supposed, by nature, more tender and loving and chaste and pure—and advocated instead women's full and equal participation in politics, work, and the arts, on the grounds that women were in every way equal to men."[4] Marston got a lot right about introducing a female character to the cohort of male superheroes. Little girls should be able to see themselves in popular culture. I think he was also right to shift away from the feminist insistence on everything being completely equal.

In Wonder Woman, Marston articulated a truth about women's sensitivity and nurturing nature that St. John Paul II expressed much more clearly fifty years later in his 1988 apostolic letter *The Dignity and Vocation of Women*: "The moral and spiritual strength of a woman is joined to her awareness that *God entrusts the human being to her in a special way*. . . . This entrusting concerns women in a special way—precisely by reason of their femininity—and this in a particular way determines their vocation. The moral force of women, which draws strength from this awareness and this entrusting, expresses itself in a great number of figures of the Old Testament, of the time of Christ, and of later ages right up to our own day. *A woman is strong because of her awareness of this entrusting.*"[5]

In the Old Testament, we learn of the patience exhibited by Sarah, entrusted with the fulfillment of God's plan by bearing Abraham a son, Isaac, after a lifetime of barrenness. Rebekah, too, bore Isaac two sons after a long period of barrenness. Both women were entrusted with building a nation. They drew strength from the knowledge that God entrusted them with his plan. The greatest example of this entrustment is evident in the Blessed Virgin Mary's fiat, her yes to God when the angel told her she would conceive a son through the Holy Spirit: "Behold, I am the handmaid of the Lord. May it be it done to me according to your word" (Lk 1:38). In the ages since, we continue to see how this entrustment, the special care of the human person, becomes the work of the saints, the pursuit of justice.

Sometimes the pursuit of justice seems contradictory. Social justice, which calls for order and the good in a society, coexists with justice for the individual, which in an ordered society may include punishment as a consequence to crime. While we might think of justice exclusively in the context of Wonder Woman fighting against evil and exacting the justice that comes from punishment, justice as a virtue includes our entrustment by God to care for other human beings. In this sense, Wonder Woman does double duty as she pursues both the establishment of order in society and the maintenance of peace for the sake of the individual.

Characters such as Wonder Woman—when they exhibit admirable virtues such as the pursuit of justice and display strength while being true to their feminine natures (what St. John Paul II calls "the 'genius' which belongs to women")— serve to encourage us to pursue the same. Marston believed women lead best because they love. Early depictions of

Wonder Woman show her using all her resources to win
battles and then returning to the scene of the battle to nurture
and encourage the victims and perpetrators alike to make
sure the victory holds. Saints often do the same, as we'll see
with St. Katharine Drexel, who wasn't content with establishing schools; she held the administrators accountable for
their success. That's justice, too, and in some cases requires
more courage than racing into battle with magic lassos.

A REAL-LIFE WONDER WOMAN

St. Katharine's story begins simply: she was born to loving
parents Francis and Hannah Drexel on November 26, 1856.
Tragically, just weeks later, her mother died. Francis, overcome with grief, left little Katharine and her older sister,
Elizabeth, with his brother and sister-in-law. A couple of
years later, Francis remarried. He brought his daughters
home to live with him and his new wife, Emma, and soon
another daughter, Louise, was born.

The girls were raised in a devout Catholic family dedicated to quietly helping the poor in their community. Francis
Drexel was a wealthy investment banker and a philanthro-
pist. Emma Drexel dedicated herself to raising their daughters to be sensitive to the dignity of those persons who
benefitted from the Drexels' philanthropic work. Francis
and Emma certainly set an example for their daughters to
live lives of service. From a young age, the girls helped their
mother with the distribution of food, clothes, and other items
to those in need in their community, and they learned this
form of love-in-action from her example of tending to the
poor with discretion. Emma's saying that "kindness may be
unkind if it leaves a sting behind"[6] no doubt made an impact
on her daughters. Her desire to protect the feelings of those

they helped created the sort of atmosphere that develops a beautiful heart for service: loving the person first and then taking care of their needs. St. Katharine puts this service in a proper context: "If we wish to serve God and love our neighbor well, we must manifest our joy in the service we render to Him and them. Let us open wide our hearts. It is joy which invites us. Press forward and fear nothing."[7]

A GROWING SPIRIT OF SERVICE

Although the Drexel sisters had been raised to have a social awareness and philanthropic spirit in the community, Katharine had the sad opportunity to practice the works of mercy in the intimate setting of their own home. Katharine's stepmother, Emma, who raised Katharine as her own, developed cancer. Katharine cared for her for the three years Emma battled the disease before it took her life. In those years, Katharine surely fed and clothed, tended, consoled and comforted, prayed for and with Emma, and finally laid her to rest in 1883.

Just two years later, in 1885, Francis Drexel died. He left his daughters an enormous inheritance for the time. Drexel arranged for his daughters to have substantial earnings from his estate, which was distributed evenly among the three sisters. This income would prove to be a boon to many organizations and charities developed by the Drexel sisters.

This period of time was instrumental in Katharine's spiritual development. She began discerning a calling to the religious life, and shared this growing desire with Bishop James O'Connor, her spiritual director. O'Connor, a longtime family friend from his days as a priest in Philadelphia, encouraged Katharine to wait before committing to the religious life. He pointed out to Katharine that she was in a unique situation to serve the poor and marginalized because of her family's position and wealth. O'Connor saw for Katharine the possibility of using her fortune as a layperson, fearing that a vow of poverty would limit her access to these funds for charitable works.

By the time the Drexel girls were women, they had traveled throughout the United States and Europe and had seen firsthand racial inequality and its effects on poverty. Katharine especially was moved by the conditions for Native Americans in the western states and pledged to financially assist some of the missions in the area, especially the St. Francis Mission on the Rosebud Reservation in South Dakota.

Drawn to the racially marginalized and poor, the sisters travelled west to visit Native American reservations and met with many members of the missions and their communities. These initial meetings led to the Drexels' financial support of those efforts, from giving endowments for building to paying salaries for teachers. They shared this vision as a family, although Katharine managed most of the work.

A SURPRISE COMMISSIONING

With both their parents dead, the Drexel sisters turned their sights on their vocations. They travelled to Europe again, and in early 1887, in a private family audience with Pope Leo XIII, Katharine requested that the pope send missionaries to the Native American reservations. Katharine had already been discerning the religious life, but the pope's response, "Why not, my child, yourself become a missionary?"[8] must have had an immense effect. She returned to the United States and resumed the conversation about a religious calling with Bishop O'Connor, who suggested she should form a congregation to serve racial minorities in the country.

By 1889, Katharine had entered the convent of the Sisters of Mercy in Pittsburgh, and her sister, Louise, had married. The next year, Elizabeth married and tragically became seriously ill while pregnant. She and the baby died in childbirth. Although grieving, Katharine and Louise found themselves with a greater portion of the inheritance and continued to dedicate themselves to the growing needs of their charitable endeavors. Katharine took her holy vows and, aided by Louise and her husband, Edward Morrell, founded the Sisters of the Blessed Sacrament for Indians and Colored People (shortened later to Sisters of the Blessed Sacrament) to serve the Native Americans and African Americans more closely.

Mother Katharine, as she now called herself, set about the business of establishing a motherhouse in Bensalem, Pennsylvania, and building up the congregation, which had grown to fourteen, including herself. The endeavor was not without difficulties; the Sisters were often targeted by people who felt they had no business working with poor Native Americans and African Americans.

Nevertheless, the need to serve in these communities was great, and Mother Katharine pressed on. Among her advisors was Mother Frances Cabrini, founder of the Missionary Sisters of the Sacred Heart of Jesus. Wonder Woman may have had the Justice Society of America to work in concert with other superheroes, but here is a real-life social justice league: two women who would later become canonized saints working together, St. Katharine Drexel and St. Frances Xavier Cabrini!

Mother Katharine would spend the rest of her life and her fortune building schools throughout the Southwest. The Sisters of the Blessed Sacrament built a school in Santa Fe, New Mexico, for Native American children and then built a school for African American children in New Orleans,

Louisiana. That school went on to become Xavier University. By the time Mother Katharine had died at the age of ninety-six, there were more than five hundred sisters in the order. They had opened more than 140 missions, nearly 50 grammar schools, and a dozen high schools. In fact, Mother Katharine's influence and generosity across the American West was so extensive that the order had difficulty accounting for everything because Katharine had begun her donations long before the founding of the Sisters of the Blessed Sacrament. Anne Butler, author of *Across God's Frontiers: Catholic Sisters in the American West, 1850–1920*, observes, "Katharine Drexel avoided vague idealism and concentrated on practical plans, devising a Catholic agenda for women reformers. She did not just talk about improving society but aggressively undertook the projects she thought would bring important positive changes—and she was not dissuaded by naysayers, regardless of their rank and prestige."[9]

Mother Katharine's legacy spread throughout the West and across several religious orders. Her financial support helped create schools to make things better for Native Americans and African Americans, and her business acumen and contacts made sure her investments in these missions and schools yielded results, even if they were small gains or for a small community. When I think of St. Katharine Drexel's impact on the lives she touched through her philanthropy, I think of our modern stewardship drives where we are called to give of our time, talent, and treasure. St. Katharine learned the importance of responsible stewardship, especially in the management of economic and human resources, as a young girl through her family's influences. She not only modeled stewardship as an adult but also instilled its value in the order of religious sisters she founded. St. Katharine perfected the virtue of justice by endeavoring to provide opportunities for the impoverished in order to improve their condition in life, thereby working for the common good.

The cause for Mother Katharine's canonization was opened in the 1960s. She was beatified in 1988 and canonized in 2000 by Pope John Paul II.

NOT SUPERHEROES BUT SAINTS

Wonder Woman espouses the ideals of a just society—a society that protects the rights and dignity of its citizens. Her battles against bad guys contribute to establishing communities where peace reigns and the common good is promoted. Unfortunately, Wonder Woman is a fictional character, and the ideal society? Well. It remains only an ideal.

This doesn't have to sound as hopeless as it appears. While we don't have a perfect society, we do have God's perfect plan for us. Each of us has a role to play in this plan—a plan for our personal salvation, and the salvation of the world. We don't need to be superheroes, but we do need a little heroic virtue. While fictional heroes such as Wonder Woman can show us what needs to be done in the world, real-life saints such as St. Katharine Drexel show us how to do it. The saints understand the world as a place to participate in God's plan.

We don't need Wonder Woman's lasso of truth, but we can follow her example to love others by working toward creating a better world for everyone. Love will accomplish much more than we can imagine when we choose to open our hearts, as St. Katharine tells us, and give of ourselves joyfully.

BEACONS
OF STRENGTH
AND LIGHT

REY AND ST. CLARE OF ASSISI

The belonging you seek is not behind you; it is ahead.

—Maz Kanata,
Star Wars: The Force Awakens

A long time ago, in what feels like a galaxy far, far away, my little brother spent his whole summer watching and re-watching George Lucas's *Star Wars: A New Hope*. He claims proudly that he saw the "Best. Movie. Ever." eleven times. Eleven! I watched it only once that summer, but to be honest, I was spending my school vacation at the beach with my grandparents; I had distractions. Forty years later, however, it's my turn to confess: I've seen *Star Wars: The Force Awakens* a bunch of times. I lost count after the DVD arrived.

What is it about this movie franchise that has so many of us holding on to these stories for decades? The answer

21

is simple: the characters are compelling. The writing has sometimes been weak—critics and fans alike complain about cheesy dialogue here and there—but the characters! The characters! There's something for everyone in these films: wise mentors, handsome swashbucklers, earnest heroes, an intelligent and courageous princess. Add loyal sidekicks and some menacing villains and you've hit a formula for success.

It's a fun adventure story that has layers of meaning. On a philosophical level, the films explore universal themes that draw us into the narrative because they strike a chord deep within us. The theme of good versus evil, manifest in the light and dark sides of the Force, works as a story element precisely because this is a battle so much a part of the human condition that it plays over and over again in centuries of history. But Star Wars is more than a story of good versus evil—it explores other themes just as important and just as human: friendship, community, redemption, justice.

The iconic opening crawl in *Star Wars: The Force Awakens* points us to the theme of justice: "Luke Skywalker has vanished. In his absence, the sinister FIRST ORDER has risen from the ashes of the Empire and will not rest until Skywalker, the last Jedi, has been destroyed. With the support of the REPUBLIC, General Leia Organa leads a brave RESISTANCE. She is desperate to find her brother Luke and gain his help in restoring peace and justice to the galaxy."

So much of good storytelling begins in the audience's willingness to suspend disbelief and buy into the events in the story. A huge part of that involves the characters. Do we like them? Do we see ourselves in these characters? Are they people we want to emulate? If we can answer yes to these questions then we jump into the adventure with both feet, living vicariously through the characters, experiencing things that sometimes form us in ways we didn't anticipate.

There's a warning in there to choose our entertainment wisely, of course, in order to make sure it supports, or at least doesn't negate, our values. But this entering into the story also brings to light the joy many women and girls experience when these larger-than-life adventure stories include female protagonists with whom to identify.

That summer of 1977, my little brother's idols were Luke Skywalker and Skywalker's mentor, Obi-Wan Kenobi. Forty years later I get to wax poetic over the heroine of *The Force Awakens*, Rey, and the return of my favorite heroes from *Star Wars: A New Hope*. Although I have always admired Princess Leia and believe she is a well-developed character in the early Star Wars trilogy who returns even stronger and more formidable in *The Force Awakens*, Leia didn't drive the action the way Luke did in the original trilogy. Princess Leia, now General Organa, leads the Resistance and gives orders, sure, and that's an impressive position of authority and a win for feminism, but she didn't carry a lightsaber, and she didn't fly an X-Wing Starfighter into the Death Star to blow it up.

In *The Force Awakens*, however, Rey steals the *Millennium Falcon*, the iconic ship belonging to Han Solo in the earlier Star Wars films. She flies the old freighter and makes her escape from Jakku, a desolate desert of a planet where she believes her family left her and will someday return. Her theft sets off a tracking device that alerts Han to the location of his beloved ship, missing for many years. Han captures the ship, and Rey and her companions, Finn and the droid BB-8. The return of the *Millennium Falcon* sets into motion a series of events that pulls Rey into a cause she tries to resist but finally joins.

I admit I am too often like Rey, slow to do the things I must do. My default is to say no to anything new or anything that will demand a commitment, so I come to things reluctantly and not without some later regret that I didn't jump in wholeheartedly earlier than I did. I catch a glimpse of some part of myself in these characters sometimes, and I think I can learn a little bit about courage from them. As with Rey, the cause sometimes seems far away from me, but the people are close, and those relationships are the first thing to pull on Rey's heart—and mine. After all, it's in relationships that we learn about love. Not just love for those close to us but love that extends outward to members of our communities and circles of influence. In turn, we desire to give others their due, whether it's aid to the poor or dignity for the marginalized.

MYSTERIOUS REY, RELUCTANT HERO

Early in the film we discover that Rey is a scavenger. Left alone on the desert planet Jakku, she demonstrates resilience, strength, intelligence, cleverness, and a flair for nonconformity and rebellion that helps her survive in this wilderness. Rey also has a deep woundedness that comes from being abandoned by her family. At the end of a day of scavenging and bartering, we see her at a grounded ship—the place she calls home. There, she seems to console herself with a small doll and a pilot's helmet—perhaps scavenged, but more likely mementos from her past.

Her wistfulness touches me in this scene, tugging at my maternal instincts. Capable, strong, resourceful—what does that mean to her if she is alone and abandoned? Her quiet contemplation here leads me to believe she is a deep thinker, perhaps a dreamer. When she dons the fighter pilot helmet, perhaps she dreams of adventure.

DREAMER AND FRIEND

The adventure comes to Rey, and it's explosive. She finds a small utility droid, a BB-8 unit that serves as a kind of rolling toolbox with an artificial intelligence interface. Unwilling to part with it, she becomes a target for the scavenger boss who wants it. The First Order has put out a seize order for the droid, and the scavenger boss, along with every shady trader in the galaxy, comes after it. In the madness of trying to escape from these goons, Rey encounters Finn, a Stormtrooper with a conscience and a flair for chivalry who has deserted his unit in the evil First Order. Finn, a gentleman, attempts to help Rey during their escape. He keeps trying to rescue her, taking her hand and protecting her, but Rey wants none of it, saying at one point, "I know how to run without you holding my hand."[1] I remember being a young woman and rebuffing the young men who showed kindness and good manners when opening doors.

Rey rejects his overtures, but Finn constantly extends the hand of friendship. He reminds Rey that that she isn't alone and tries to show her she is part of something greater. Rey rescues Finn from the First Order. They flee hit men and Imperial Troops, escaping in the salvaged *Millennium Falcon*. However, it is really Finn who does the rescuing. Rey has been alone for so long she only knows how to be alone, but this slowly changes with Finn's friendship. Finn saves Rey from herself by constantly challenging her and opening her to new relationships that are built upon values other than barter and trade. They don't know it yet, but *together* they will do their part to restore justice to the galaxy.

The *Catechism of the Catholic Church* identifies this need for community: "In keeping with the social nature of man, the good of each individual is necessarily related to the common good, which in turn can be defined only in reference to the human person: Do not live entirely isolated, having retreated into yourselves, as if you were already justified, but gather instead to seek the common good together" (CCC, 1905). Part of seeking the common good is rooted in justice. Giving each person what he or she is due creates an environment that is rich in opportunity for individuals to flourish. This is not about the distribution of goods or material things but rather the promotion of an environment that protects the human dignity of each member of the society.

Rey and Finn's encounter, rooted in survival, flourishes because they offer what the other needs. Rey's solo status changes when Finn inserts himself into her life. He brings her into community, first by befriending her and then by staying by her side as they join the Resistance. Rey, in turn, values Finn as an individual. The anonymous uniformity of the Stormtroopers stripped Finn of his humanity. Rey's growing friendship with him demonstrates that she values him. In giving each other their due and their value as persons, the duo is better able to take on the challenge to defend the peoples oppressed by the New Order.

CHOSEN TO LEAD

Rey and Finn experience freedom for a brief time before Han Solo and Chewbacca capture the *Millennium Falcon* from them. Han is being chased by the First Order as well as by the traders he and Chewbacca swindled. Together, Rey, Finn, Han, and Chewbacca escape to a planet where Han has a contact: Maz Kanata. Impressed with Rey's flying abilities and her instincts, Han offers her a job, but she declines, wanting to go back to her home planet in case her family returns. Maz Kanata, a known pirate and friend of the Rebellion, offers a temporary haven to the four fugitives but challenges Rey's identity: "Who are you?" she asks. Rey responds, "I'm no one."

"No one." That statement struck me so powerfully. Here is a young woman with no identity. Rey has no last name. Abandoned on Jakku, she missed the warmth and love of a family that would make her *some*one. Rey has never experienced being a beloved daughter. She has no family to give her a sense of belonging. No wonder she resists everything. It's not just that she knows only what it's like to be alone; it's that she doesn't know how to be in community.

Although she rejects Han Solo's job offer, the Force seeks her. The dark side finds her and attacks through the First Order, and the light side beckons her through an unexpected artifact: a lightsaber. Maz Kanata reveals the significance of the lightsaber: "That lightsaber was Luke's, and his father's before him, and now, it calls to *you*."

Rey wants no part of this, but she's already quite deep into the adventure. Fear. Hesitation. Insecurity. Maz might have seen any of those emotions on Rey's face and responds gently but with conviction: "I am no Jedi, but I know the Force. It moves through and surrounds every living thing. Close your eyes; feel it. The light, it's always been there; it will guide you. The saber, take it."

Despite having an affinity for the Force, Rey seems frightened of its power and rejects the lightsaber, exclaiming, "I'm never touching that thing again. I don't want any part of this!"[2] When Maz removes the goggles she wears so she can get a closer look at Rey, we see a gesture of compassion as well as exhortation. She respects Rey's response but hands the lightsaber to Finn for safekeeping until Rey accepts her destiny.

Rey shows incredible depth here, as she allows her fears to get the best of her and runs away, even after having exhibited courage multiple times during her escape from Jakku. The lightsaber shows her the past when she first touches it, and she relives her abandonment on Jakku. She also witnesses a terrible massacre scene in that moment. She recoils and rejects the saber—perhaps rejecting the Force. We don't know. In fact, there is very little that we do know about Rey, but that's part of the adventure in the story: the discovery of Rey's true identity.

IDENTITY: WHAT'S IN A NAME

Names are important. Naming a character in a work is often an intentional act designed to give the readers—or, in the case of films, the viewers—some kind of symbolic clue as to the nature of the character. The name emphasizes or communicates essential elements of the character's personality and gives us hints about what we can expect from her.

In *The Force Awakens*, Rey encompasses the hope for the future of the Republic and hints at a future for the Jedi Knights, but who is Rey? At the end of the film we have no clearer idea of her identity than we had at the beginning. Yet there is a clue in her name. *Rey* means king or ruler in Latinate languages. Speculation that Rey may be heir to the Skywalker family suggests that she has a legitimate claim to the lightsaber. If we consider the homophone of Rey to be ray, as in light, then Rey becomes the embodiment of light and the light side of the Force.

Rey struggles with her identity throughout the film because she doesn't know who she is or where she came from. She believes that she is no one. Nevertheless, Rey's ownership of Luke Skywalker's lightsaber hints at her identity as a Jedi. She has been in the dark, so to speak, for most of her life, and now that she is awakening she begins to see she may have a role beyond self-preservation.

The Jedi's mission is to protect peace and justice in the galaxy. In *The Force Awakens*, we see Rey's transformation from self-centered survivor to warrior and defender of the common good. She moves in small steps as her awareness grows. First, she rescues Finn, then fights alongside Han Solo and Chewbacca, and finally joins the Resistance movement. Her final step in the film is filled with hope.

Playing around with names and symbols is what I do as a student of literature. It enhances my appreciation for a text and uncovers layers of meaning, whether intentional or accidental. However, naming human persons is no game. In fact, it is a sacred act that eternally ties the person to God: "God calls each one by name. Everyone's name is sacred. The name is the icon of the person. It demands respect as a sign of the dignity of the one who bears it" (*CCC*, 2158).

The *Catechism of the Catholic Church* explains this deep connection between our names and our identities: "A name expresses a person's essence and identity and the meaning of this person's life. God has a name; he is not an anonymous force. To disclose one's name is to make oneself known to others; in a way it is to hand oneself over by becoming accessible, capable of being known more intimately and addressed personally" (*CCC*, 203).

In Baptism, we are baptized in the name of the Father and the Son and the Holy Spirit, and our names are given. Through this sacrament, we become daughters and sons of God. Regardless of the circumstances in our lives, this is our new identity, our eternal one. While I've always known my personal identity, and known that through baptism I became the adopted daughter of God, the deeper understanding of that kinship and identity came to me late in life. Whereas I did things to please my earthly parents when I was young, as was expected of me, I now want to please my heavenly father and pursue those things pleasing to him. My parents helped me to develop virtues that God, through his grace, helps me perfect.

Rey is, after all, a fictional character, but how many people, in failing to recognize their true identities, have felt a kinship with her hopelessness? Films such as this sometimes encourage us to be introspective and lead us to deeper thoughts about our identities, the meaning of our lives, and even our vocations. This kind of introspection may lead us to better understand our roles as active participants in God's salvation.

THE VALUE OF LOVE

Although Rey and Finn start off their relationship with conflict, they soon become good working partners, even friends. Finn doesn't intend to stick around once they get off Jakku, but after the First Order attacks and captures Rey, he returns to the Resistance base to share information about the First Order weapon and provides key information about the base. In yet another moment of altruism, he attempts to rescue Rey, who has (resourceful woman that she is!) already freed herself. Unfortunately, that escape leads to a last battle with the film's villain, Kylo Ren, and in a last ditch effort, Finn once again comes forward to defend Rey and is severely wounded.

In a tender moment at the end of the film, Rey visits the unconscious Finn, gives him a chaste kiss, and whispers, "We'll see each other again. I believe that."[3] There was a lot of speculation about the nature of Rey and Finn's relationship following the release of the movie. Maybe it's romantic;

maybe it isn't. It's worth noting, however, that Rey isn't given an overtly romantic interest in this film. This is unlike trends in earlier Star Wars films, where the heroines, Princess Leia and Queen Amidala, both pursue justice *and* romance. Maybe romance is also in Rey's future, but for the moment, her focus remains on basic survival and her growing investment in this family of warriors that has taken her in.

Han Solo, especially, expresses admiration and respect for her in classic Solo style when, on the way to a skirmish, he hands her a weapon:

> *Han Solo:* You might need this.
> *Rey:* I can handle myself.
> *Han Solo:* That's why I'm giving it to you!

Han's delivery, complete with smirk, also comes across as proud of the young woman, and this gesture speaks of Han's confidence in Rey's abilities. Rey, orphaned and abandoned, responds to this small but significant instance of spiritual fatherhood from Han Solo. Though the scope of this book focuses on women and heroines, we must recognize the importance of men in our lives, too, especially as they contribute in positive, healthy relationships.

Unfortunately for Rey, the enemy is too powerful. Kylo Ren, the villain in this film, reads Rey's mind when he captures her and learns of her growing attachment to Han Solo. Han Solo is Ren's father. Once a powerful Jedi-in-training, Ren was seduced by the Force's dark side and left, leaving his parents, Han and Leia, bereft. Now a Dark Lord, Ren torments Rey, suggesting that Han Solo will disappoint her in the end.

In a tragic turn of events, Rey witnesses the battle of wills between Han Solo and Kylo Ren. Han comes face-to-face with his son, reaching deep into Ren's heart to find what's left of the light in his son's soul. Ren seems to be responding, but ultimately, overcome by the dark side, kills his father. Rey, who has lost everyone in her life, witnesses the murder.

The next time Rey sees Kylo Ren, she summons the light side and uses the lightsaber to battle against him. Rey's affinity for the Force, still undeveloped, becomes apparent to her and others. She aligns herself with her new friends and chooses to fight on the side of peace and justice.

SEEKER OF JUSTICE

The enduring theme of the Star Wars films is the triumph of good over evil, the eternal battle of the light versus the dark sides of the Force on a galactic scale. The films also explore this theme on the smaller though no less epic scale of the individual human person. As Christians, we're reminded that we must act, whether singly or in concert with others, according to God's plan for salvation in our lives.

In Star Wars we see the seductive nature of the dark side. In spite of lessons learned in the Skywalker family, Darth Vader's legacy is that his own grandson, Kylo Ren, succumbs to the allure of the dark side. But Ren's situation is not without hope, either, as Darth Vader himself sought and found redemption at the end of his life. Individuals continue to fight, alone and collectively, to promote the best possible society for all. Thus, Star Wars's theme of good versus evil is also a story about the universal quest for justice.

Rey first needs to understand her own dignity as a person and recognize that dignity in others, thanks to Finn's example to her, before she is able to move away from fighting for her own personal survival to fighting for justice. When she finds this conviction, perhaps in that moment when she loses a father figure in Han Solo, she is able to turn herself over completely to the cause of Good. This newfound sense of responsibility sends her on a new mission dedicated completely to this quest for the good, for the light. Rey's maturity in accepting this responsibility shows seeds of the Catholic Church's teachings on this quest: "The dignity of the human person requires the pursuit of the common good. Everyone should be concerned to create and support institutions that improve the conditions of human life" (CCC, 1926). Recognizing this change in Rey, General Leia Organa sends the young woman in search of Luke Skywalker with the final words to this installment in the story: "May the Force be with you." In this commissioning, Leia hands the lightsaber found earlier at Maz Kanata's to Rey, a symbolic passing of the baton to a new generation and a sign of hope for all the galaxy as Rey seeks the last living Jedi Knight and defender of the good in the galaxy.

ANOTHER RAY OF LIGHT, ST. CLARE OF ASSISI

St. Clare of Assisi was born to a wealthy father and a pious mother in 1193, a time of turmoil throughout Italy. Wars between regions and cities were common. Power and wealth were wielded like weapons, which led to tension even in those places where there was a tenuous peace. Little is known about Clare's early years. However, one legend states that when her mother was carrying Clare in the womb, she heard a voice while at prayer. The voice consoled Clare's mother, saying the child would be a brilliant light in the world. This light would be a theme throughout Clare's life, and she would later write about it, saying, "Rejoice always in the Lord and do not allow yourself to become involved by any darkness or bitterness."[4]

Clare's life was spent in the light—seeking the Lord in everything she did. When she was eighteen, Clare had a profound conversion while attending the homilies preached by St. Francis of Assisi. She committed herself to a life of poverty, rejecting the riches and comfort of the life she had at home. On Palm Sunday in 1212 Clare went to the church where Francis was preaching and consecrated herself to the Lord. She dedicated herself to Christ secretly, not out of shame but to do so away from the objections of her father, who wanted her to marry according to his wishes. He found out anyway and tried to physically remove her from the church, but she was indomitable, holding onto the altar and resisting until her father gave up and went away.

A RELUCTANT LEADER

Francis removed Clare to Sant'Angelo, a Benedictine convent in Panzo, some distance away from Assisi, to protect her from her angry father. Francis was working on the San Damiano chapel, adding a monastery there. When the work was completed, he sent for Clare, and appointed her abbess of the monastery. She was reluctant, but Francis insisted, calling upon her vow of obedience. At age twenty-one, Clare took on the leadership of this growing Order of Poor Ladies of San Damiano. They became known as the Poor Clares, and she was their Mother for the rest of her life. She served the sisters and the Friars Minor for forty years.

Following Francis's dramatic renunciation of worldly goods, Clare adopted an austere poverty, refusing to own anything, whether personally or in community. The Poor Clares went barefoot, slept on the floor, and begged for their food. They abstained from meat, and Clare included other mortifications such as constant fasting, which caused Francis to intervene for the sake of her health. Clare eventually became ill and spent the last several decades of her life infirm. In spite of poor health, she served the sisters and friars unfailingly, with love and in love.

Every act of service was an outpouring of this love. Although Clare was the abbess and ostensibly in a position to lighten her physical load, she continued to serve as one with her community, often tending to the sick and frequently tending to the sisters who went into the community begging. Those, especially, received tender care from their Mother, who washed their feet and served them when they returned.

SPIRITUAL FRIENDSHIP AND THE LIGHT OF CHRIST

As a young woman, Clare saw a world that needed Christ's tender mercy, and she wanted nothing more than to live a spiritual life with zeal, on fire for the Lord. When she heard Francis preaching, she knew she had found someone with this same zeal. She found in Francis not only a teacher but, more than that, a friend.

Clare was the first woman to approach the friars with an interest in following their ways. When she poured out her heart to Francis, finding in him a spiritual brother, he accepted her. So great was Clare's conviction that tradition tells us Francis gave her his own tunic and rope for a belt. Not only was she the first woman to enter this Franciscan community but she was also the first woman to ever draw up the rule for an order.

Clare's commitment to Francis's vision of poverty caused some conflict with two popes. First, Pope Gregory IX absolved the Poor Clares from a vow of poverty in order that they should own the property where they lived in community. He felt this was necessary to protect them. Clare appealed to him to change this, and he relented. However, upon Pope Gregory's death, his successor, Pope Innocent IV, reinstated the clause to allow property ownership, sharing the late pope's concerns about the women's vulnerability. Clare once again appealed to a pope to allow the sisters to stay true to Francis's vision. Just days before Clare's death, Pope Innocent approved Clare's new rule forbidding ownership at the convent in San Damiano.

Clare's desire to honor Francis reveals the importance of his influence in her life. Their spiritual friendship serves as an example to all of us of the role of friends in our lives and of how to grow in love for each other and the Lord: "The friendship between these two saints is a very beautiful and important aspect. Indeed, when two pure souls on fire with the same love for God meet, they find in their friendship with each other a powerful incentive to advance on the path of perfection."[5]

Legend has it that one night Clare and one of her sisters joined Francis at the Portiuncula church for dinner. Their presence emanated such a bright light that it was seen for miles around. When we are in love with the Lord, it is impossible to tamp down his radiant love.

The imagery of light, purity, and love are deeply associated with Clare, whose very name speaks of clarity and light. Pope Innocent IV, in his bull *Gloriosus Deus*, which promoted her canonization, addresses her as "O Clare, endowed in a manifold manner with titles of clarity."[6] This clarity of mind and heart comes from understanding the source of all, that is, faith in Jesus Christ. One of the remarkable miracles attributed to this profound faith is rooted in Christ's presence in the Blessed Sacrament. One night, the convent came under siege by Saracen invaders. Clare, already infirm and weak, placed a monstrance within view of the invaders and prayed, "Does it please Thee, O God, to deliver into the hands of these beasts the defenseless children whom I have nourished with Thy love? I beseech Thee, good Lord, protect these whom now I am not able to protect." The Saracens withdrew and turned their attention to the city of Assisi. Clare, not satisfied with their own safety, turned to her sisters to pray and fast through the night to save the city, too.

St. Clare was canonized in 1255, just two years after her death—a remarkable testament to the holy life she led.

THE PURSUIT OF JUSTICE

Both the fictional Rey and the canonized St. Clare of Assisi share some common experiences. We know little of their youth; their public lives begin in their late teens as they enter adulthood and must make choices about where to lead their lives. Both, as it happens, choose to follow the way of light, Rey in the fictional Force and Clare in Jesus Christ. There's also the accidental connection of their names to light! A bonus for this lover of words and word play.

Both women, too, become reluctant leaders, as Rey takes on the calling from the Jedi tradition and Clare accepts leadership of her order as lifetime abbess. They also respond to the encouragement and direction of a close friend: Rey learns about friendship through Finn, and Clare's spiritual friendship with Francis yields much fruit for them personally, for the Franciscan Order, and for subsequent generations.

Finally, Rey and St. Clare serve as models of justice for today's world. The *Catechism of the Catholic Church* defines justice as the "virtue that consists in the constant and firm will to give . . . due to God and neighbor" (*CCC*, 1807). We see this virtue in a fictional character who works to uphold the common good. Through St. Clare, we learn about the value of humility. Through her loving service to her sisters and the Friars Minor, we see a woman who puts her whole self at God's service, all done for the love of Christ Jesus.

Where Rey gives her due to neighbor, St. Clare demonstrates the will to give her due to God as Psalm 29:2 exhorts, "Give to the LORD the glory due his name. Bow down before the LORD's holy splendor!" We see the seeds of this justice in the fictional Rey, but true inspiration comes from St. Clare, who, as a flesh and blood woman, gives witness to the immensity of and yet simple recipe for justice, which is to love God and all his works, even embracing poverty to do what is right.

PUTTING JUSTICE INTO ACTION

Our relationship to our neighbor is bound up with our relationship to God; our response to the love of God, saving us through Christ, is shown to be effective in our love and service of people. Christian love of neighbor and justice cannot be separated.

For love implies an absolute demand for justice, namely a recognition of the dignity and rights of one's neighbor. Justice attains its inner fullness only in love. Because every person is truly a visible image of the invisible God and a sibling of Christ, the Christian finds in every person God himself and God's absolute demand for justice and love.

—World Synod of Catholic Bishops,
Justice in the World, 34

1. Look around in your circle of family and friends. Is there someone who could be showered with your love? Maybe this person could use a supportive word. Perhaps he or she is in need of something you can help provide. Act.

2. Identify a project for the poor or marginalized in your community that can use a donation of your time, talent, or treasure. Give freely and with love.

3. Find a local church that offers Adoration and spend some time with the Lord.

4. Ask someone if you can pray for him or her. If you are comfortable, ask for their intentions. Then, of course, pray!

PART II

★

SEEKING
PRUDENCE

Of the four cardinal virtues, prudence might be the least understood. Or perhaps, the most misunderstood. It has nothing to do with being a prude, and everything to do with being perceptive.

The *Catholic Encyclopedia* defines prudence as "an intellectual habit enabling us to see in any given juncture of human affairs what is virtuous and what is not, and how to come at the one and avoid the other."[1] The key word, *habit*, suggests that we need to work at this as a skill. It can be learned. The problem with that, in my experience, is that anything that requires work first requires commitment. In other words, I need to decide to work on this virtue and then actually practice it. And practice some more. Invariably, I'm going to fail and have to start all over again.

By the way, recognizing that when we fail we should pick up the mess and start again is prudence. Funny how that happens!

The *Catechism of the Catholic Church* describes it like this: "*Prudence* is the virtue that disposes practical reason to discern our true good in every circumstance and to choose the right means of achieving it; . . . it guides the other virtues by setting rule and measure. . . . With the help of this virtue we apply moral principles to particular cases without error and overcome doubts about the good to achieve and the evil to avoid."

In other words, we use prudence to help us make choices—to make the good or morally right choice. It's a habit we develop over time, so we must work at it every day.

The heroines in this section, Natasha Romanov and Dana Scully, demonstrate prudence in their careful analyses of their choices. They've made bad choices in their lives that have led to grave errors and sin, and they have adjusted their mindsets to change their behavior. St. Mary Magdalene demonstrates a supernatural prudence, the grace to keep her gaze on Jesus all along when those around her focus on his death. St. Teresa Benedicta of the Cross applied rational thinking to overcome her disbelief. St. Mary Magdalene and St. Teresa Benedicta of the Cross had to overcome trials to arrive at holy dispositions.

IMPARTERS
OF MERCY
AND SERVICE

BLACK WIDOW AND
ST. MARY MAGDALENE

If it's the last thing I'll do on Earth, I'll make it some-
thing good.

—Natasha Romanoff, *Black Widow #19*

It's hard to imagine that Natasha Romanoff better known
as Black Widow from Marvel's Avengers comics, could have
any interest in doing a good deed. She's a secret agent, a spy,
and a cold and calculating killer by training. The idea that
there could be a desire to turn her evil skill set to use for the
benefit of humanity surprises me; that she could have a soft
spot for one person after a lifetime of monstrous acts piques
my curiosity. Why the change of heart?

Evil was the easy route in Natasha's life. She worked on automatic pilot, doing her job and not worrying about the effects of her actions. Her eventual choice to avoid evil and defend the good came at a great price for her as she was immediately marked as a defector and a traitor, as untrustworthy and irredeemable. Faced with this reality, she joined SHIELD, an organization that employs a variety of people to maintain order in a world overrun with evil and threats from other universes. She explains the change: "Before I worked for SHIELD, I, uh, well, made a name for myself. I have a very specific skill set. I didn't care who I used it for or on."[1] Natasha notes that she has lost a lot in her life and realizes she has a great debt caused by all the harm she once did, a debt she is unhappy to be carrying.

Through SHIELD, Natasha attempts to atone for the terrible things she has done in her life. Loki, an evil ruler from another universe, challenges Natasha on her heartless past and what he believes to be futile attempts to change her ways.

> *Natasha Romanoff:* It's really not that complicated. I've got red in my ledger; I'd like to wipe it out.
> *Loki:* Can you? Can you wipe out that much red? . . . Your ledger is dripping, it's *gushing* red, and you think saving a man no more virtuous than yourself will change anything? This is the basest sentimentality. This is a child at prayer. *Pathetic!* You lie and kill in the service of liars and killers. You pretend to be separate, to have your own code. Something that makes up for the horrors. But they are a part of you, and they will never go away![2]

Natasha doesn't accept Loki's assessment of her remorse. She has, in fact, turned her life around. She has rejected the impulsivity and violence of her past. She has found in SHIELD an organization that she can stand by and has found friends, the Avengers, who will support her.

Now Natasha uses that very special skill set to defend Earth and protect lives, lives she once took with no compunction and no remorse. SHIELD opened up the possibility for relationships based upon mutual respect. It opened up the possibility for love.

The absence of love in Natasha's earlier life certainly left her wounded. After a lifetime of intrigue, lies, and cover-ups, she shares with Bruce Banner—better known as the Hulk and another member of the Avengers—the intimate details of her training, including, sadly, her forced sterilization:

> *Bruce Banner:* Natasha, where can I go? Where in the world am I not a threat?
> *Natasha Romanoff:* You're not a threat to me.
> *Bruce Banner:* You sure? Even if I didn't just—there's no future with me. I can't ever—I can't have this, kids, do the math, I physically can't.
> *Natasha Romanoff:* Neither can I. In the Red Room, where I was trained, where I was raised, um, they have a graduation ceremony. They sterilize you. It's efficient. One less thing to worry about. The one thing that might matter more than a mission. It makes everything easier. Even killing. [*She hesitates.*] You still think you're the only monster on the team?[3]

Natasha grows in this friendship and intimacy with Bruce Banner because she has made a conscious choice to leave behind her past and embrace a future that is filled with hope. It may be a future that has none of the traditional comforts of a family and children, but it is a future that is as far away from death and that Red Room as possible. She

speaks of the relationships she has found within the Avengers, especially with Banner: "Fact is, he's not like anybody
I've ever known. All my friends are fighters. And here comes
this guy, spends his life avoiding the fight because he knows
he'll win."[4]

Natasha's attraction to Banner complements her choice
in prudence, to carefully consider her actions in order to
make the choice that best supports the good. Banner's ability
to control the Hulk, while not always a successful endeavor,
speaks to his commitment to nonviolence. When he does
choose to fight, it's because there is no other way to protect
society or his friends. Both Banner and Natasha are willing
to consider other options before resorting to violence. This
inspires me to approach the unexpected in my life with prudence, and carefully consider the implications of my actions
before responding.

We see a subtle change in Natasha throughout the Marvel movies. Although she has already aligned herself with
the good guys when we first meet her in *The Avengers*, over
time her character grows in complexity as we discover her
personal story and her pain. She finds in Bruce Banner a
kindred spirit who ignites hope. These are the characters
that engage me, the ones that have some hidden pain or bro-
kenness that must be overcome on their quest for the good.
When I see characters who have turned around their lives
for good, it encourages me when I find myself in a cycle of
sin. I can begin again, too.

The tender exchange between Black Widow and the
Hulk after the battle of New York shows an unafraid Natasha Romanoff humming a lullaby to calm him. She carefully,
lightly, touches his hand and then his wrist to get him to
focus on *her* instead of the destruction surrounding them.
This simple act of trust beckons Bruce Banner to emerge from

the depths of the Hulk's monstrous shell. Natasha doesn't see a monster. Instead, she accepts this alter ego on equal terms as her friend, Bruce.

This scene captures a moment of intimacy between two heroes whose initial purpose in life rendered them killing machines. Natasha was bred for espionage and murder. As a small child, she was taken into a school for girls where she learned to be an assassin and a spy. She was stripped of everything—her family, her identity, and even her fertility. All of that was taken away from her, leaving an angry young woman with a fierce gift for hand-to-hand combat and murder. Bruce Banner, on the other hand, suffers at his own hand. A physics experiment with weaponry goes awry when a young man stumbles in the way, and Banner takes the brunt of powerful gamma radiation to save the youth. The blast radically alters Banner's physiology. Now when Banner gets angry or fearful, he transforms into an out-of-control, hulking creature.

While the Hulk inspires fear in his opponents because of the sheer magnitude of his size and rage, Black Widow's strength resides behind the facade of an unassuming young woman whose bite is both subtle and deadly. Her small, delicate frame juxtaposed against the wild ferociousness of the Hulk makes this scene after the battle all the more tender as she trusts Bruce with her life. She endangers herself to save her friend. The sweet lullaby plus the small hand in the gigantic one paints a picture of love where these hands, once used to kill and destroy, are now open to life and possibility.

The deeply moving truth in this display—Natasha's vulnerability at the hands of Hulk—speaks to her growing love for the man. She is willing to risk her own life to help save his. I didn't expect to find such a rich illustration of scripture in the midst of a blockbuster film, but the scene captures the magnitude, and magnanimous nature, of love: "No one has greater love than this, to lay down one's life for one's friends" (Jn 15:13). This understanding of love acts as a recurring theme in the Marvel universe and reinforces the value of friendship and filial love. We learn through these characters the importance of building strong relationships.

I love that the tools of destruction, their hands, also become vehicles for building new relationships.

Our hands do important work, whether they bear the scars of heavy labor in fields or construction, the steadiness necessary in technical applications, or the soft caresses of lovers. Our hands bear witness to our lives. What I saw in my husband's hands was part of what attracted me to him from the beginning—I saw a man willing to work hard for his dreams, a man who could and would work hard for those he loves. Perhaps that's too much for a young woman to surmise from a young man's hands. Then again, maybe we respond viscerally to a lot of things around us that we can understand before we put those thoughts to words. After all, it was the calming touch of Natasha's hand and not words that stilled the beast Bruce Banner had become.

Their relationship, a burgeoning love story in the Marvel universe of blockbuster movies, touches me because it is a story of redemption. These two dangerous, volatile people find a reason to change the way their lives are going, however unlikely that may seem, in order to pursue the good in the world. The Hulk could no longer give in to his anger and continue to rage, causing nothing but destruction in his wake. Natasha, too, was tired of living a life isolated from all consequences.

NOT JUST ONE OF THE GUYS

While some people are frustrated that Black Widow is the only female member of the Avengers, I'm sold on the idea of Black Widow as the only woman in the group because I grew up with a band of brothers, a little gang of kids that ran up and down the neighborhood fields while our mothers took care of our younger siblings. Like Natasha, I was the only girl in the group. I learned to climb trees, run fast, hit a ball, and terrorize squirrels with firecrackers. I'm not all that proud of the last thing, but it was the sixties—firecrackers and little boys usually meant shenanigans were afoot, and I was along as one of the guys.

Of course, that changed pretty suddenly when I was about twelve or thirteen, but up until then I played and fought alongside my own group of Avengers. Although things did change for me over those next years, I still felt more comfortable with the boys. But I also liked to see myself represented in the action stories I was drawn to. Even now, as an adult, I revel in the fact that Natasha can hold her own with these heroes and that she does it without any supernatural powers, just training and the will to do it.

Natasha has a heroic virtue that drives her spirit, and I'm drawn to that. I don't fear alien invasions, but I do work hard in my vocation as wife and mother to protect those I love, and to provide a comfortable and healthy life for them as best I can. On most days, my work around our home comes easily to me. I'm living the dream of retirement after thirty years in the classroom, teaching. That means a slower pace, but there's still a pace. I mean, I haven't figured out a way for the laundry to get done on its own. In fact, I haven't figured out a way to make sure the laundry lands in the laundry basket. (Remember that guy with the manly hands? He has lousy aim when he's not interested.)

So what does a mild-mannered retired college professor see in the wild and dangerous Black Widow?

Intentionality.

Natasha Romanoff, a woman who was forced into becoming an exceptional spy, chose to walk away from that life and apply her skills to seeking peace and good in the world. It wasn't a casual decision; it was a choice. And it's a choice that she continues to make throughout the movie franchise, especially in *Captain America: Civil War* when the Avengers group splintersovertheir personal and political beliefs. Natasha uses reason to make an intellectual analysis of her actions. She studies the facts, determines the best course of action, and then executes what she believes to be the *correct* course of action.

She acts prudently.

That's a pretty courageous thing to do—a heroic thing, in fact, because she's faced with opposition even from within the ranks of the Avengers.

It takes a courageous woman to stand up for her beliefs because it's the right thing to do.

My active imagination enjoys movies that show courageous women who do the right thing because I live vicariously in the excitement and adventure. The six-year-old me that ran around with sticks bent as bows and jumped out of trees pretending to fly loves these adventures. But now, I enjoy going over these movies and discussing them with friends. This is where the characters really show up as role models, as we break down the characters, analyze their actions, and try to discover their motivation.

I enjoy making sense of characters' behavior in light of how my actions echo theirs. The juxtaposition helps me refine my own thoughts on important matters and discern how best to tackle the difficult things in my life. It may seem odd at the outset, but I admire Black Widow.

Natasha Romanoff's approach to problem-solving aligns itself with the cardinal virtue prudence. I'd venture to say that's not a word most people would associate with a spy, fictional or not, but she has the right combination of detached observation and reasoning ability to draw conclusions effectively. That doesn't necessarily make her good or moral; it just makes her smart.

But Natasha does draw conclusions that lead to good moral choices. She can, when weighing the evidence in front of her, make the distinction between right and wrong, good and evil. That distinction tips the scale from simply being a good analyst to making good moral choices. It is not enough to know the difference between good and evil; one must also want to be good. One must also want to act in a way that supports the good. Natasha not only makes the distinction between right and wrong, but she also has the courage to make the right choice and to act according to that choice.

Some people might say this is just having a conscience. It took Black Widow a long time and many missteps to develop that conscience, but she did. You might say it saved her. Did she wreak havoc along the way? She did more than that—atrocities she committed still weigh heavily on her heart, things she doesn't name because they are so awful they are lumped together as red on her ledger.

I can understand that. I certainly have plenty of marks in my ledger that I wish I could erase. Mistakes. Errors. Intentional acts against others and myself. Against God. Dare I say *sins*?

I am a sinner. Admitting that helps me see the behaviors, identify them, and make changes that help me avoid them

in the future. It is the first step toward learning the prudence
to act correctly.

While Natasha Romanoff helps me see the possibilities
for redemption as it plays out larger than life on the big
screen, it's easy to dismiss prudence as too difficult. I'm not
a heroine in a movie with writers who have the power to tip
the scales in my favor with the flourish of a pen. I'm human,
living in a world fraught with distractions and temptations.
And evil. Let's not for a second deny that there are forces
working against us. They might not be aliens or monsters,
but they are real.

I take heart from women who, living in the real world,
fight and win battles against these forces of sin. St. Mary
Magdalene stands out as one of those heroines. I admit I
bought into the scandalous nature of her depiction as a prostitute and, honestly, didn't move beyond that label. Sure, I
knew she was a saint, but I fell into the ease of the label and
didn't look into the remarkable story of her life for a very
long time. What a shame for me. As much as I like Black
Widow, I have come to love St. Mary Magdalene.

Now *there's* a real badass saint.

WHAT DID THEY CALL HER?

The story I knew about Mary Magdalene when I was growing up was part heavily edited by my catechism teachers and
part cultural confusion from the then-popular rock opera
Jesus Christ, Superstar. Add to that the recent confusion from
The Da Vinci Code and cable television tell-alls that place
Mary Magdalene in hypothetical scenarios, and you have
everything I knew about this saint. Oh, and that she was
possessed by seven demons that Jesus cast out of her. That
part is indisputable.

But truth, as they say, is stranger than fiction—and the rest of the story of this remarkable woman gives me pause. There aren't volumes of information and history about her, but her presence in key moments of Jesus' life point to a woman who knew the truth of the Resurrection before anyone else. Before even the apostles! That is no small thing.

First, though, let me clear up some confusion about who I thought Mary Magdalene was and what scripture tells us. We know she had demons cast out of her, but she is often depicted as a repentant prostitute. St. Mary Magdalene suffers a bit from an identity issue. Sometimes she's confused with Mary of Bethany and other times with the unnamed sinful woman who washed Jesus' feet with her own tears (see Lk 7:36–50). When you consider just how many women named Mary were in Jesus' life, it's easy to see how there could be some confusion with stories jumbled together.

I can understand that. I've often joked that every Hispanic girl I knew in school was named Maria. Many of us are—which is why in intimate circles I answer to my middle name. I don't have to go outside the family to illustrate—one of my husband's uncles has five daughters, all named Maria-*Something*. I'd hate to be the guy calling one of these sisters. "I'd like to speak with Maria." Talk about a comedy of errors!

So to pin down Mary Magdalene as definitively any of the women named Mary in scripture has led to some traditional interpretations that remain with us today. One of these traditions is often referred to as the "composite" Mary Magdalene because several stories are merged to create a persona, including the one about perfuming Jesus' feet. That's where the notion of Mary Magdalene as a repentant prostitute emerges. It's further reinforced in the list of patronages she holds: converts, hairdressers, penitent sinners, perfumeries, and sexual temptation, among others. In art, she is often depicted with very long hair and holding an amphora, perhaps the vial of perfumed oil from Luke's account that was saved to anoint Jesus after his burial.

As a professor of literature, I have a great appreciation for legends and myths because they illustrate meaningful concepts. St. Mary Magdalene's popularity, once grounded in scripture, grew into legend and myth. Like Black Widow, who had a past too sinful to bring up, the Mary Magdalene persona that emerged in the Middle Ages depicted a repentant prostitute who also has a heavily sinful past. This is where metaphor as a storytelling vehicle teaches us some of the beauty of our faith.

Pope Gregory the Great, in a homily delivered circa AD 591, says this about the "composite" Mary Magdalene:

> She whom Luke calls the sinful woman, whom John calls Mary, we believe to be the Mary from whom seven devils were ejected according to Mark. What did these seven devils signify, if not all the vices? It is clear, that the woman previously used the unguent to perfume her flesh in forbidden acts. What she therefore displayed more scandalously, she was now offering to God in a more praiseworthy manner. She had coveted with earthly eyes, but now through penitence these are consumed with tears. She displayed her hair to set off her face, but now her hair dries her tears. She had spoken proud things with her mouth, but in kissing the Lord's feet, she now planted her mouth on the Redeemer's feet. For every delight, therefore, she had had in herself, she now immolated herself. She turned the mass of her crimes to virtues, in order to serve God entirely in penance.[5]

In this analysis, Pope Gregory the Great pairs the seven demons with the seven deadly sins and then, for each sin, a corresponding atonement that matches the crime, so to speak. It reminds me, in form, of Peter's denial of Jesus three times on the eve of the crucifixion. Later, Jesus asks Peter three times, "Do you love me?" He gives Peter the opportunity to replace each no with a yes. It's a beautiful moment for Peter to recover from his shameful behavior. Whether or not Mary Magdalene is the woman in the story, the effect is the same. We are afforded by Jesus Christ, in his mercy, the opportunity to make right our wrongs. Mary Magdalene recognizes her salvation is in Christ and acts upon it. While this may initially appear to be an emotional response rather than a well-reasoned one, Mary Magdalene had actively sought Jesus, especially during the most dangerous periods of affiliation with him. She demonstrates detachment from the world and its punishments, and clings to the Lord.

This is the Mary Magdalene that corresponds to the Black Widow—both are women with pasts so sinful, so reprehensible, that they fear to even hope for redemption. Both Natasha and this Mary Magdalene walk away from lives of sin. Their sinfulness isolated them from the possibility of relationship with others. Natasha Romanoff seeks the opportunity to do good things in order to wipe the red from her ledger, and the sinful Mary seeks the opportunity to wipe the transgressions from her soul. They are each offered salvation: one from a man as broken as she and the other from the Son of God, broken by man to redeem us. Mary Magdalene's commitment to Jesus, her presence and witness to his passion and death, might have left her bereft. Yet she remained by his tomb, even when the others left. If we judge Mary Magdalene by our worldly definition of prudence, we might say she behaved in the exact opposite of the virtue.

It was reasonable for the Apostles to go home, or at least leave the grave to pursue the good things demanding their attention. However, Mary Magdalene demonstrates a supernatural prudence that is fixed on Jesus Christ, the best good. This dedication was rewarded by being the first witness to his resurrection.

WILL THE REAL MARY MAGDALENE PLEASE STAND UP?

So who *is* St. Mary Magdalene? She is mentioned a dozen times *by name* in the New Testament. That alone is worthy of note. However, when and where she is when she is named makes her all the more amazing, amazing enough to be called the Apostle to the Apostles by St. Thomas Aquinas because she was the one who brought the news of the Resurrection to the apostles.

* ★ Both Luke (8:2) and Mark (16:9) note that Jesus cast out seven demons from her.
* ★ In the same vein, Luke (8:3) mentions she, as well as other women, provided for the needs of Jesus and the apostles.
* ★ She was present at the crucifixion (see Mt 27:56, Mk 15:40, and Jn 19:25).
* ★ She witnessed Christ's burial (see Mt 27:61 and Mk 15:47).
* ★ She went to Christ's tomb on Sunday morning and discovered his body missing (see Mt 28:1–8, Mk 16:1–8, Lk 24:1–7, and Jn 20:1).
* ★ She encountered the Risen Christ and, after speaking with him, ran to tell the apostles (see Mt 28:9–10, Mk 16:9–11, and Jn 20:11–18).

St. Mary Magdalene was the first person to see Jesus after the Resurrection and recognize him. Can you imagine being the one to announce to everyone that Jesus is risen? Oh, to be the bearer of such news! And yet she was met with incredulity by some of the apostles.

But why Mary Magdalene? There were other women around. Certainly, there were apostles and other followers. We can look at Mary Magdalene's presence with Christ as an indication of her commitment to him and her dependability in such a situation. We know from the scriptural accounts that after her healing from the demons, she not only followed Jesus but also provided for him from her own means. She followed Jesus to his death on the cross. She helped bury him. She returned to care for his body. Mary Magdalene, I would think, would know Jesus if she saw him.

Mary Magdalene would act prudently. Assess the situation. And she did. She had persevered in staying by Jesus's side. Her joyful response to being called by name might appear impulsive. However, if prudence is the virtue that helps us attain the good, which is God, then Mary Magdalene's response epitomizes prudence in not only recognizing but also concretely acting to adore the Lord. She didn't need any proof other than being called by name by her beloved Jesus Christ. We, too, are called by name.

This encounter with Christ, according to Pope Benedict XVI, "lets us experience all God's goodness and truth, who frees us from evil not in a superficial and fleeting way, but sets us free radically, heals us completely, and restores our dignity."[6] St. Mary Magdalene, who was once possessed by demons, is healed by Christ. She was lost to the world through the bondage of possession and set free by Mercy himself.

I admire Natasha Romanoff's desire to make up for the evil she has committed and seek the good. I aspire to St. Mary Magdalene's confidence to seek *and find* the Lord. Although her story in scripture is incomplete, the part we know to be true, her witness to the Risen Christ, fortifies my faith.

PARAGONS OF
WISDOM AND TRUTH

AGENT DANA SCULLY AND
ST. TERESA BENEDICTA
OF THE CROSS

*Anyone who seeks truth seeks God, whether
or not he realizes it.*

—St. Teresa Benedicta of the Cross

FBI agent Dana Scully of the television series *The X-Files*
runs with high heels. I can't say that impressive skill, prob-
ably augmented by the art of a good film editor, sets her
apart as an exceptional special agent, but I admire it all the
same. Although this ongoing wardrobe schtick garnered
some wry commentary from fans, it's Scully's persona that
I love. Just as I found a role model in Lt. Uhura when I was
a little girl, Dana Scully encouraged scores of girls to enter
STEM (science, technology, engineering, and mathematics)
careers, many in positions related to law enforcement and

investigation. This influence even has a name: the Scully Effect.

Agent Scully's insatiable drive and curiosity account for her success—attributes admirable in any role model. Although a medical doctor, Scully chooses to pursue a career in criminal investigation and brings her scientific methodology to the cases. As a result, she is usually involved in autopsies and toxicology reports, often working around the clock to gather the scientific information first and then apply it to the investigative process. Agent Scully, it seems, could have been a one-woman show, but she wasn't. Her assignment to debunk Agent Fox Mulder and his claims of extraterrestrial and paranormal incidents consumes her as much as the pursuit of the paranormal consumes Agent Mulder. They become a formidable team against the shadow government that seeks their destruction.

Their cases, unexplained and often ridiculed by their superiors at the FBI, end up in Mulder's basement office, because they are relegated to the FBI's most unwanted agent. Scully steps up to the challenge of solving the strange cases and, in the process, embarks on a mission to seek the truth behind the mysteries. Scully is driven by reason that demands evidence. She is prepared to accept the outcome, but she will not draw a conclusion based on whimsy or emotion. Scully needs to weigh all the evidence and pursue scenarios to plausible conclusions before committing to a course of action. What she doesn't count on is her personal journey toward truth.

Mulder's iconic poster of a flying saucer with the bold caption, "I want to believe," frames Scully when she first encounters him. The poster came to be associated closely with Mulder, but this early shot acts as foreshadowing for Scully's character development. As much as the paranormal is Mulder's cause, Scully seeks her own truths; her seeking culminates in a return to her Catholic faith after a near-death experience. Scully, the skeptic who applies a rigorous scientific methodology to Mulder's wild imaginings, wants to believe, too.

The small cross Scully wears, a gift from her mother, is an ever-present reminder that what she is seeking has been with her all along. Although Scully's faith is firmly entrenched in science at the beginning of the series, she will eventually believe in more.

SCIENTIST AND BELIEVER

There's a lot to love about Dana Scully. She's smart, compassionate, dedicated. She's also flawed in the way that we're all flawed because we are human—because we are sinners. We see that side of Scully, too. But we also see that her loyalty to Mulder defines her throughout the series, in the movies, and in a poignant way, in the special tenth season produced in 2016. Loyalty binds Scully to Mulder. Although she was originally sent to debunk his theories and thus discredit him as an agent, Scully takes on the challenge of debunking Mulder while refusing to be a pawn to the anonymous men who placed her in this assignment. In order to do that, Scully clings to her science and methodology. Science and reason will prove the truth.

This loyalty to learning the truth through science and reason costs Scully a great deal over the course of the series as she refuses to compromise in her search for the truth. She is kidnapped, given cancer, and has her eggs harvested. She gets abducted by aliens and put in cryogenic holding, gives birth to a son after being told she is infertile, and most notably, becomes a believer. The journey reveals a woman who began as a skeptic believing in science ruled by reason instead of faith ruled by the heart. In the end, Scully finds a reconciliation: science and faith are not mutually exclusive.

Scully's goal is to reach an understanding of the mysterious, the unexplained, and even the miraculous. She may struggle with the idea of aliens and the far-fetched nature of Mulder's musings, but she wants to believe in the possibilities and that the science she leans into will provide her with the answers she seeks. However, she never fully rejects religion. In fact, the stranger the events, the more open she becomes to discussing her own doubts until she finally opens up to a Catholic priest: "As much as I have my faith, Father, I am a scientist trained to weigh evidence, but science only teaches us how, not why."[1]

She does begin to reconcile religion with science. Scully comes to trust that the scientific approach can sometimes substantiate the impossible. If science can't explain it, there is still an explanation to explore:

> *Scully:* I . . . believe in the idea that God's hand can be witnessed. I believe he can create miracles, yes.
> *Mulder:* Even if science can't explain them?
> *Scully:* Maybe that's just what faith is.[2]

In a letter to the director of the Vatican observatory, St. John Paul II cautions us against making errors in creating aberrations of both science and religion, writing, "Science can purify religion from error and superstition; religion can purify science from idolatry and false absolutes. Each can draw the other into a wider world, a world in which both can flourish."[3] But it is, explicitly, aberrations that Scully investigates. Her cases push the limits of the natural world in ways that are more often than not distortions of reality. Scully and Mulder seek monsters: manifestations of evil, fairy tales, and fantasy. And yet, Scully seeks proof that these are somehow grounded in the natural order. She battles against the superstition behind these scientific anomalies but often faces a truth science refutes.

SEEING IS BELIEVING

Even the casual *X-Files* viewer recognizes the tagline "The Truth Is Out There." Almost every episode opens with that theme, perhaps an encouragement for Agents Mulder and Scully to persist in their work, but also for viewers to persist in our journeys toward the truth: "Man tends by nature toward the truth. He is obliged to honor and bear witness to it: 'It is in accordance with their dignity that all men, because they are persons . . . are both impelled by their nature and bound by a moral obligation to seek the truth, especially religious truth. They are also bound to adhere to the truth once they come to know it and direct their whole lives in accordance with the demands of truth'" (*CCC*, 2467).

Shows such as *The X-Files* speak to the seekers within us. Scully appealed to me because I discovered her at a time in my faith journey when I was filled with doubts. Like Scully, I never lost my cultural attachment to Catholicism, but I struggled mightily, as Scully did, with reconciling what I could see with what I felt. Although St. Thomas was chastised for needing to see to believe when Jesus rose from the dead, I have great compassion for him, as I too struggled with reason overriding everything else before me.

At the end of the series when Scully is called upon to present her findings, her final say on the matter of belief echoes St. Thomas: "I've seen things."[4] I've seen things, too. Like Scully, I wore a small cross, not letting go of the last symbol of my dormant faith. I wanted to believe, too.

WE'RE NONE OF US ALONE

In my postcollege years, I didn't actively disbelieve in God, but I did passively ignore his presence in my life. Church attendance went from casual to not at all. And prayer? What was that? Prayer was a discipline as much as a conduit for a relationship with God, and I had chosen not to have that relationship.

Today I would call my apathetic behavior *ghosting*, just like the trend to fade away from friendships by not returning texts or calls. I flat out stopped responding to God. I stopped attending Mass. I stopped praying. I stopped being obedient to Church teachings *that I knew to be right and good*. I stopped considering God a presence in my life.

God, on the other hand, never ghosted me. The Holy Ghost seemed to always be present in my life. In those years we celebrated births and baptisms in the family. Were these baptisms a cultural decision made out of expectations rather than conviction? Yes. But I also believe that the Holy Spirit, as we're more inclined to say today, used those first sacraments for my children to begin the work of conversion in me. Baptisms led to sacrament preparation classes when they were older. When my daughter began sacrament preparation and learned about reconciliation and communion, I found myself in the difficult position of having to explain to my children why I didn't go to Communion.

My no to God had to be turned into a yes for the sake of my children. For my sake.

Just as Scully could not ignore the empirical evidence she found in her analyses, I was having a difficult time ignoring God's presence in my life. My parents persisted in inviting me to Mass, never judging me or getting angry. Years later, as I reflect through the lens of faith, I would understand that the Holy Spirit was moving my heart. I was taking small steps toward a renewed faith—perhaps, for the first time in my life, an authentic faith.

I found inspiration in a quote by St. Teresa of Avila, a mystic I long resisted despite (or perhaps because of) a multigenerational devotion to her within my family. The happy news is that I did give St. Teresa a chance—and often, when dealing with matters of faith, that's all we need to do. I had been trying to figure out everything on this journey of faith by myself. St. Teresa, who knew a thing or two about being independent and strong-willed, offered this powerful reflection: "The feeling remains that God is on the journey, too."[5]

Of course, I was never alone, even when I thought I was. Friends and family cared for me, and God was always there. In retrospect, though, that fear of being alone drove me to declare that I chose to be alone. I had fallen easily into believing I could trust no one but myself. Interestingly, the lesser-used *X-Files* tagline "Trust No One" points out the utterly sad and despairing nature of such a notion. Dana Scully *did* trust. She trusted Mulder, and that led her on a journey of self-discovery.

I started a journey to learn about myself, too, as I dug deep to understand my Catholic faith.

RECONCILING THE FACTS

I can't quite credit Dana Scully with my reconversion to the faith; I feel that process was underway years before the premiere of the series, with the birth of my children. Even though I'm somewhat reluctant to give credit to a fictional character for encouraging my own spiritual journey, I'm not quick to completely discount Scully's influence, either. Stories often help us explore ideas and feelings. Scully's story, while not exactly mine, was close enough for me to live vicariously through her.

To my surprise, this story became a catalyst for deep thought about my own search for truth. Inspired by these personal musings, and undoubtedly by the influence of the Holy Spirit, I made a fledgling examination of conscience. As my children were entering CCD and sacrament preparation, I took baby steps alongside them. By the time my oldest made her First Confession, I had returned to the sacraments.

For Dana Scully, her return to faith happened in the third season episode "Revelations," when she and Fox Mulder are called on a case where murder victims all have in common a faked stigmata. The agents identify the last potential victim, a boy who apparently has a real stigmata or at least, as far as Scully is concerned, wounds that resemble the stigmata, right down to an unexplained cut on the boy's rib cage. The murderer is caught before he harms the boy; however, Scully is moved by the inexplicable wounds she tends while the boy is in her custody.

At the end of the episode, Scully checks in on the boy, who tells her they will see each other again. The implication for Scully is that their meeting will be in the afterlife. The interchange prompts Scully to seek out a priest; she has too many questions about the nature of miracles and, interestingly, the nature of God's mercy and forgiveness. We learn, through her confession, that it has been six years since her last confession. She fears that there might be things that are unforgiveable.

God's mercy is infinite. The scene in the confessional served a greater purpose than just as a moment of character development for Scully. It served to remind us that nothing we do is unforgiveable if we have contrite hearts. It's good to see this reminder, even if it's in a television drama. Perhaps especially if it's in a television drama. Seeing a beloved character return to the sacrament of Reconciliation after years away from the sacraments, while true to the character's development, may have also served as a small, unintentional piece of catechesis for the viewers.

My return to the sacrament of Reconciliation coincided with Scully's return. Coincidence? God-incidence? The Lord works in mysterious ways, as we're fond of saying. It is *The X-Files*, after all.

IN SEARCH OF THE TRUTH

The X-Files followed two kinds of storytelling in its long run. The independent stories told weekly, often referred to as the monster of the week, explored a paranormal event that the agents investigated, with Agent Mulder often certain the answer was in the paranormal and Agent Scully increasingly unable to use science to back up her skepticism. The other stories, personal arcs woven across various seasons, centered on a continuing storyline, such as the alien abduction of Mulder's younger sister when they were children or the menacing secret government omnipresent in the series. The personal story arcs that featured Scully pulled me in immediately.

Scully sought the truth of her existence, her identity, her purpose in life. As a Catholic, she knew the answer, but it took a near-death experience to open herself up to the possibility that she needed God. In the episode titled "*Memento Mori*" (a Latin phrase meaning "remember you will die"), Scully learns she has cancer. In a beautiful voice-over revealing her journal, Scully expresses to Mulder how their four-year relationship, as colleagues and friends, has pushed her to believe.

Scully, for the most part, is searching for the truth precisely because she feels lost. The depths of her despair as she faces her mortality bring her to the realization that perhaps she does need God. God as Comforter. God as Consoler. God as Savior. Ultimately God as Truth: "The desire for God is written in the human heart, because man is created by God and for God; and God never ceases to draw man to himself. Only in God will he find the truth and happiness he never stops searching for" (*CCC*, 27).

Scully is afraid of the truth in many ways. On the one hand, she wants confirmation that the work she has done for so many years has uncovered the deep secrets harbored by mysterious men who only operate in the dark. She fears for the safety of her son, whom she has put up for adoption in the hopes of protecting him from this evil cabal. She fears for her safety and Mulder's, too. Often, she fears God. She was most afraid, she shares with her priest in confession, that God wasn't listening to her prayers.

Mulder became her touchstone. Their work became her purpose, and together they fought for good to triumph over evil. That battle often revealed truths they were unprepared to hear. Still their disappointments and fears didn't deter them from the task. Mulder and Scully's integrity in pursuing these truths exemplify what Pope Benedict XVI says about the importance of prudence, that reason-driven decision that seeks what is right: "Prudence demands humble, disciplined and vigilant reason that does not allow itself to be dazzled by prejudices; does not judge according to desires and passions, but seeks the truth—even uncomfortable truth."[6]

Mulder and Scully could be the poster children for uncomfortable truths. I've dealt with my uncomfortable truths for a good portion of my life, and it's not limited to those first few moments in the confessional before the grace of the sacrament takes over and you're liberated by the truth. In the daily grind of living, there are small and large truths that, when revealed, make me uncomfortable, that can make anyone uncomfortable.

Perhaps we are faced with a situation where we must charitably correct a family member or dear friend. Maybe a situation at work requires that we remove ourselves from a project that is morally offensive. Our social activities could need recentering so that they are healthy and conducive to Christian growth. These situations and others require us to make decisions or, as St. Augustine suggests, "a right distinction between what helps it toward God and what might hinder it."[7] Our actions should move us toward the good, not away from it.

Prudence is not an easy virtue to form, but like so many other things, the continuous practice of it makes the process easier. We're never experts; rather, we continue in its practice, moving toward God all the time. We can do this in small steps, such as choosing friends who will support and encourage our values instead of devalue us, eating a healthy diet, getting rest and exercise, participating in the sacraments, making decisions to support a healthy and prosperous family life, recognizing our need for reconciliation, and openly pursuing a relationship with the Lord because it is the right thing to do.

THE TRUTH HURTS

One of the most interesting saints to come out of the twentieth century exemplified great prudence in her handling of her conversion to Christianity from Judaism.

St. Teresa Benedicta of the Cross, sometimes still called by her birth name Edith Stein, captivated me right away. The very first thing I read about her centered on St. Teresa of Avila. *No way*, I thought, *St. Teresa of Avila is pretty busy knocking sense into people!* It must have made quite an impact— while visiting a friend, Edith picked up the autobiography of St. Teresa of Avila and became engrossed in the book. Upon completing the volume, she declared that she had finally found the truth she had been seeking. Thus began her conversion to Catholicism.

The truth Edith found in that book not only set her on the path of conversion but it also set her on a completely different course for her life. She felt such an affinity with St. Teresa of Avila that Edith also felt called to the Carmelites. That would prove to be more difficult than her baptism into the Catholic faith. Both Edith's conversion and her entrance into the Carmel at Cologne, Germany, a dozen or so years later were vehemently opposed by her mother. Sadly, signs of a possible reconciliation toward the end of her mother's life by way of small notes came too late, and her mother died before a full reconciliation. St. Teresa of Avila wrote that "to have courage for whatever comes in life—everything lies in that."[8] Edith would need to hold fast to this advice from her new spiritual heroine.

KINDRED SPIRITS

I felt overwhelming sympathy for Edith's decision to enter the monastic life and what it would cost in her relationship with her mother. It's never easy to be separated from loved ones. When it's a personal decision, there can be feelings of rejection and abandonment. It's not surprising that Edith's mother responded with hurt feelings.

Just as Edith decided to join the Carmelites, my parents made the difficult decision to leave Cuba for the United States. My parents pursued what they believed to be their calling for their family. They longed for an opportunity to live in peaceful safety, to openly worship, to live free. This came at the high price of isolation and separation from loved ones.

I recently reconnected with family in Cuba after a fifty-year separation. I left Cuba in October of 1965 and returned fifty years later, almost to the day. My return to Cuba during Pope Francis's Missionary of Mercy Apostolic Visit in 2015 opened the doors to reunion and reencounter. There was no need for reconciliation. Our separation, while difficult, was a suffering of absence, not rejection. There was no animosity, just love and goodwill. That love and goodwill thrived for decades as we prayed for one another across the Florida Straits. But it could have gone another way—the way of hurt and rejection. I'm grateful to have been raised in a family that understood the power of prayer and the pull of family ties.

Edith must have suffered because of her mother's rejection, but she also felt the pain of causing her mother grief. She put this separation into a new light—the opportunity to pray for those in the world. The cloistered life in the Carmel separated her from her family, but Sr. Teresa Benedicta had these consoling words regarding the Carmelite vocation: "Those who join the Carmelite Order are not lost to their near and dear ones, but have been won for them, because it is our vocation to intercede to God for everyone."[9] I can't help but think all of us can meet at this bridge of prayer. Perhaps her mother came to understand that at the end. I know my own family has experienced the graces from intercessory prayer.

THE SEARCH FOR TRUTH

Edith Stein's story begins in Breslau, Germany (now a part of Poland). She was born on October 12, 1891, the youngest of eleven children. Her father died when she was just a toddler. Her mother raised her in the Jewish faith, but by the time Edith was a teenager, she started to disregard the religious practices she had been taught. Prayer was quickly abandoned, and by the time Edith was in college, she was as far removed from Judaism as she could be.

Edith became a student of philosophy. Not only did it challenge her religious upbringing and introduce new ways to think about the universe but it also taught her how to reason. It also opened up in her a yearning for answers. St. John Paul II, years later, would explain how we are disposed to this yearning, "Faith and reason are like two wings on which the human spirit rises to the contemplation of truth; and God has placed in the human heart a desire to know the truth—in a word, to know himself—so that, by knowing and loving God, men and women may also come to the fullness of truth about themselves."[10] After years of searching for the truth, Edith had her own epiphany: she recognized her need for God. No wonder she wanted to act quickly when she believed she had found him after reading about St. Teresa of Avila. Edith was baptized Catholic the following year! However, her desire to enter the Carmelite Order was delayed, largely because of her spiritual director's prudent advice to slow down.

Edith's mother was profoundly affected by her daughter's conversion. It wasn't enough that Edith had abandoned the faith for so many years; that she converted to Christianity was a painful blow. Edith's delay in entering the Carmelites was as much a consideration for her mother as it was an opportunity for her to mature in the faith before making such a profound commitment. Prudence called for a plan that would be charitable toward her mother, who purportedly wept at the news of her daughter's conversion, and that would honor the sense that Edith had work to complete before she could enter religious life.

In those years leading up to her conversion and then waiting for the opportunity to enter the Carmelites, Edith served the Lord by using her skills as a teacher and philosopher. Her philosophy training, which once led her toward atheism, now led her to God and could be used to lead others to God, too.

A beautiful part of Edith's story during those years spoke to my teacher's heart. Her spiritual advisors told her to continue her work—philosophy was her gift, and that, too, served the Church. Her skills as a teacher trained many future teachers.

I often felt a measure of guilt that I had gone to work in the public school system instead of teaching in a Catholic school. A kindly priest put me at ease by encouraging me to teach where I found myself. He told me my work was in teaching the students with love—something I've taken to heart. Edith did the same over the next twelve years. She continued teaching, spending years living among Dominican sisters. She also continued her work in philosophy and completed a translation of St. Thomas Aquinas's work *Quaestiones disputatae de veritate*.

Edith was gaining a reputation as a well-respected Catholic speaker, and she addressed in particular the question of women in the workforce. Decades before the mid-twentieth-century feminist movement took hold, Edith Stein declared, "There is no profession which cannot be practiced by a woman."[11] Being a woman did not hinder her work. Unfortunately, her Jewish heritage did.

TRUTH AND CONSEQUENCES

Eventually, Edith was pushed out of her teaching position. It was 1933, and the powerful National Socialist government in Germany had gained ground with the persecution of Jews. Edith knew that she would be facing hardships. The time was right for her to enter the Carmelite monastery in Cologne, Germany.

I've lived in Europe twice in my life. Both times I was what Sheldon Vanauken, in his memoir *A Severe Mercy*, called "a happy pagan." I had no idea of the rich Catholic heritage that surrounded me, but in spite of myself, I experienced a number of places that today are meaningful to me. I spent some time in Cologne, and even though the city was rebuilt after almost total destruction during World War II, I walked along some of the paths St. Teresa Benedicta must have walked when she arrived at the Carmel in Cologne.

My years in the Bavarian town of Bamberg gave me an opportunity to experience a memorial of *Kristallnacht*, the night of November 9, 1938, when SS soldiers destroyed synagogues and the personal property of thousands of Jews. It was a violent night filled with beatings in addition to the destruction of homes, businesses, and places of worship. It was an example of violence I was unfamiliar with even though I had read history books and spoken to people who had firsthand knowledge of the Nazi horrors. My friends and I joined the community leaders and citizens as we walked in silence that night, stopping at residences and businesses in the old part of town, some of us to pray, others to reflect—a stark contrast to the violence perpetrated on an innocent people almost fifty years before.

Now known as Sr. Teresa Benedicta, she fled these horrors in Germany and went to live in the Carmel at Echt in the Netherlands. Her sister Rosa had converted to Catholicism and made her way to the Netherlands to be close to her. Their mother had died, spared the atrocities that would befall her daughters. By early 1942, Sr. Teresa Benedicta had been identified as Jewish and forced to wear the yellow Star of David by the Nazi forces occupying the Netherlands. That summer, in retaliation for a pastoral letter from the archbishop of Utrecht, who condemned the persecution of Jews, the Nazis rounded up all religious who were born Jewish and later baptized Catholic and sent them to the concentration camp in Auschwitz, Poland.

When the SS soldiers came for Sr. Teresa Benedicta and Rosa, the sisters went peacefully. Her last words at the Carmel were addressed to her sister, Rosa: "Come, we are going for our people."[12] In this final act she offered up her immediate suffering for her people, the Jews. Sr. Teresa Benedicta never gave up her identity as a Jew and, in fact, once said that she never felt more Jewish than when she discovered Jesus Christ: "I had given up practicing my Jewish religion when I was a fourteen-year-old girl and did not begin to feel Jewish again until I had returned to God."[13]

Sr. Teresa Benedicta died at Auschwitz in 1942, no doubt within days of arriving. Pope John Paul II canonized her on October 11, 1998.

TRUTH TRUMPS FICTION

I'm an avid fan of conspiracy shows such as *The X-Files*. When I taught literature at a small liberal arts university, my favorite topics concerned the human condition. We read epic stories of human suffering with heroines rising to triumph against the odds. We discussed characters in depth, celebrating their virtues and discussing their merits as role models.

Mulder and Scully are a study in virtue. Scully, as a scientist, uses reason to arrive at a course of action that protects the good. She models prudence in her use of reason to arrive at the truth. She fascinates me both because of her faith and, obviously, because she is a woman in this traditionally male role of special agent for the FBI.

Scully suffers isolation because of her beliefs and her increasing support for Mulder. Her world is turned upside down because of her affiliation with Mulder, and her family is endangered and harmed. For years, Scully labors to ensure that good would triumph over evil, whether it is in solving a crime, taking down a shadow government, or finding the truth that so eluded her. In the end she loses everything. Except her faith.

But Scully is a fictional character in a fictional world designed to entertain us.

To discover Edith Stein—St. Teresa Benedicta of the Cross—as a flesh and blood woman who experienced real-world isolation, discrimination, and horrifying torture inspires me. St. Teresa Benedicta's life is a sobering account of one woman's deeply personal encounter with Christ—her conversion to Catholicism after seeking and finding the truth within the very field of philosophy that initially led her to atheism.

St. Teresa Benedicta's courageous life and valiant death completes a heroic journey that comes full circle. The heroine experiences a call to action, an initiation, and a return to her beginnings. Edith suffered a separation from her family after her conversion to Christianity and gave herself completely to Christ in her Carmelite vocation. While her death at the hands of the Nazis came for the simple reason that she was Jewish, St. Teresa Benedicta accepted her death as an opportunity to be on the Cross with Christ. She bore her suffering,

she said, as expiation for sins: "I accept the death that God
has prepared for me in complete submission and with joy as
being his most holy will for me. I ask the Lord to accept my
life and my death . . . so that the Lord will be accepted by
his people and that his kingdom may come in glory, for the
salvation of Germany and the peace of the world."[14]

Pope John Paul II called St. Teresa Benedicta of the Cross
a confessor of the faith and a martyr. I would add that she
was a twentieth-century heroine.

PUTTING PRUDENCE INTO ACTION

> The prudent man, who strives for everything that
> is really good, endeavors to measure every thing,
> every situation and his whole activity according to
> the yardstick of moral good. So a prudent man is not
> one who—as is often meant—is able to wangle things
> in life and draw the greatest profit from it: but one
> who is able to construct his whole life according to
> the voice of upright conscience and according to the
> requirements of sound morality.
>
> So prudence is the key for the accomplishment
> of the fundamental task that each of us has received
> from God.
>
> —St. John Paul II, General Audience, October 25, 1978

1. List some words that express prudence. Does changing
the vocabulary give you a better grasp of this virtue? How?

2. Write a definition of prudence in your own words. Name
one step you can take that will help you refine this virtue
in your life.

3. Name some of your favorite fictional characters that exhibit prudence. Why do these characters resonate with you? Do you find that you share characteristics with them, or are they role models you would like to emulate?

4. Think of saints that demonstrate prudence. How does this virtue help them grow in holiness? How can you apply the same to help you grow in holiness?

5. Reread the above excerpt from St. John Paul II's General Audience. You can also find the full text online at the Vatican website. The excerpt concludes with the statement that we must all work to complete the task we have each received from God. Think about what that task might be. Ultimately, it is to participate in our salvation, but ponder the role prudence has in that plan. How will you strive to create and perfect the habit of this virtue?

PART III

★

SEEKING
FORTITUDE

Fortitude, you might say, is a fancy way of saying courage. So why not say courage to begin with? Well, it's a little matter of finesse. When we talk about courage, we think about the heroes in this section, for example. Storm, from the X-Men, is courageous, as she battles daily against the forces of evil in the Marvel Universe. Hermione Granger from the Harry Potter series also has courage. She beat up a troll; punched Draco Malfoy, the school bully, in the nose; and faced the most evil wizard of all time, Voldemort. Their brand of courage includes bravery and physical strength. However, when we consider why they are acting courageously, we discover a selfless motivation for the common good.

Using the word *fortitude* rather than *courage* gives the virtue gravitas. Let's look at Merriam-Webster's definition of fortitude: "strength of mind that enables a person to encounter danger or bear pain or adversity with courage." There is a moral component that makes fortitude weighty and worth having: "*Fortitude* is the moral virtue that ensures firmness in difficulties and constancy in the pursuit of the good. It strengthens the resolve to resist temptations and to overcome obstacles in the moral life. The virtue of fortitude enables one to conquer fear, even fear of death, and to face trials and persecutions. It disposes one even to renounce and sacrifice his life in defense of a just cause" (CCC, 1808).

St. Cunegunde and St. Marguerite d'Youville had fortitude. Talk about conquering fear of death and facing trials and persecution! St. Cunegunde walked across hot irons and wasn't even hurt. St. Marguerite endured verbal and physical abuse for years until her good work in the community was recognized. That's fortitude!

GUARDIANS
OF DIGNITY
AND CULTURE

STORM AND ST. CUNEGUNDE

You counter despair with hope. You strive forever for the best you are capable to be! Therein lies the victory!

—Storm, *Heroes for Hope: Starring the X-Men #1*

Storm, a human mutant, is primarily associated with the X-Men team and the Avengers in the Marvel Universe. Her mutant power, the ability to harness the weather and to fly, makes her one of the most powerful of the mutants. This subspecies of the human race carries a mutated gene that either accentuates or develops a superhuman power in those born with the mutation. Accidental exposure from experiments in the Manhattan Project caused mutations in the general population. As a result, mutants can be present at any level of society; they appear fully human and, in many cases, hide their mutations out of fear or shame.

Most mutants, like most people, want the common good. However, there are some who misuse their powers for personal gain, and others whose self-aggrandizement leads to evil. Storm joins forces with other X-Men to battle evil in the world, often mutant against mutant. Sometimes she unites with other forces, such as the Avengers, to battle threats against humanity. Storm's character, and the mutant universe, introduces an important theme to the otherwise good-versus-evil tropes of superhero stories.

The mutants invite us to ponder the topic of human dignity. Mutants are born to human parents and exhibit all the characteristics of human beings, plus an exceptional trait caused by a mutated gene. Often, the mutation results in a physical change: wings, fur, claws. Other times, the traits are not easily discernable: mind reading, time travel, the ability to shape-shift. As a result of these changes, the mutants stand out in the mainstream crowd. Their "otherness" becomes a focal point. Fear and misunderstanding leads to ostracism, and in some cases the mutants have self-mutilated to remove their visible differences. Nonetheless, they are fully human and deserve the same dignity afforded all persons. The X-Men, in particular, address this theme in many of their comics because it fits well within the fictional universes that were created as a reaction to social themes when the comic book genre rose to popularity.

The development of the comic book superhero in the early part of the twentieth century came about as a response to evil in the world, manifested by the atrocities of world wars. Superheroes became supernatural solutions to the world's ills, but the storylines maintained the truth of the human condition and the mess humans are capable of making when the desire for wealth or power becomes disordered. Storm makes this clear to fellow mutant Wolverine when she states that their purpose as X-Men is to protect life.

The superheroes bring order. Typically, the stories involve one superhero, a superman or wonder woman. We accept the hero as an exception—as a rare and special being among us. The mutants, however, introduce the idea that we are surrounded by beings who have this element of "other," and this "otherness" makes us uncomfortable.

The mutants make up a significant portion of the population, but they are marginalized, misunderstood, and often unwanted. Scientists, both human and mutant, work to isolate and remove the mutations, starting a war between humans and mutants. While some mutants welcome the cure and want to be "normal," others rage against the offense to their dignity. They don't want to be changed, and they resent the implication that they are not whole or valued as unique individuals with worthwhile contributions to society. This story arc becomes the basis for much of the conflict in these superhero stories, persistently raising the question of whether we eliminate mutants because the technology exists to accomplish it.

It is a frightening development as old as the atrocities in the early twentieth century perpetuated by those who believed eugenics to be a real science, but its relevance in the Marvel Universe mirrors much of the conflict in today's society. The mutants symbolize any of the marginalized in society because the "other" almost always has an element of being dehumanized first: the poor, the immigrant, the ethnic or racially different, the outsider. Storm and the X-Men can be added to that list. She recognizes that to be human is to fall short of perfection, saying, "We are . . . damaged goods—that is part of what makes us human,"[1] and she lives to protect that vulnerability in the human race.

The themes in these storylines courageously touch upon topics that are difficult and often divisive: Is it acceptable to abort or euthanize a mutant? Is it ethical to change a mutant and remove the characteristic that makes her unique? The X-Men dare to make us examine how we respond to the "other" in our society by posing these challenges in the fictional world, but they carry over into reality. They question actions in the human world such as terminating pregnancies based on perceived handicaps or judging people based upon their appearance. These comic book stories, so often dismissed as light children's entertainment, have matured into an adult medium for self-examination in the tradition of good literature.

Storm's creators, writer Len Wein and artist Dave Cockrum, responded to a recommendation in the 1970s by editor Roy Thomas to add a female character to the X-Men in order to add diversity to the all-male Marvel lineup. She debuted with a striking look and an equally compelling backstory. Ororo Munroe, later named Storm, is the daughter of a Kenyan tribal princess and an American father. She is born in Harlem in New York City but moves to Cairo, Egypt, while her father pursues work there. Her parents are killed tragically, leaving the young Ororo to fend for herself in the streets of Cairo.

Ororo falls under the influence of a gang leader and becomes a thief. She encounters Professor Xavier, leader of the X-Men, when she attempts to pick his pocket in the market. He recognizes that she is special, a mutant, but loses sight of her for many years. Ororo eventually leaves Cairo, pulled to the south to regain her bearings. She travels to Kenya, where she feels she belongs, and encounters Ainet, who becomes a spiritual mother to her. Ainet teaches Ororo with loving kindness, and the young woman begins to discover the breadth of her powers. One day, Ororo, sad to see the effects of drought on her village, summons rain to ease the suffering in her community. Her actions demonstrate great compassion and caring, but the cost of her compassion is the creation of an imbalance in the weather system that leads to drought in other villages.

This well-meaning action causes strife for others. Ainet gently guides Ororo, teaching her to control the impulse to act without considering the consequences. Thus begins the formation of Storm's conscience—the real discipline of her superpowers. She emerges as a kind of rain goddess in the community until she is recruited by Professor Xavier to join the X-Men. Storm brings to the team the all-encompassing power of the storm, tempered by serenity and kindness. She also demonstrates a gift for leadership and almost immediately rises to the position of deputy leader of the X-Men.

Storm's superpowers make her one of the strongest mutants in the universe. Her ability to manipulate the weather extends beyond making storms. She can alter weather patterns, bring up or dissipate atmospheric events, and manipulate the wind to carry her in flight. Notably, her emotions sometimes produce changes in the weather, too. All of this indicates both her close relationship with nature and the power of her will. As a result, Storm is less susceptible to mental manipulation by mutants with psychic abilities.

MARKED WITH AN X

Storm's greatest virtue is her fortitude. When she was orphaned at age six, she took to the streets and learned how to survive in a hostile world. She demonstrated fortitude again by leaving that life behind her as she pursued the good. This admirable change came with sacrifice, and it allows Storm the vulnerability to be influenced by Ainet's teachings. It takes fortitude, an ongoing commitment to endure difficulties, to change the direction of one's life and to face the old demons and stand by with integrity. She stands up to Professor Xavier, her new mentor and leader, when he tries to capitalize on her old skills: "I will fight for you. Someday, I might die for you. But do not ever ask me again to steal for you, Professor Xavier. I am an X-Man, and we have to be better than that."

Committed to the good in her work with the X-Men, Storm rises in the ranks and eventually becomes the leader of the X-Men. In the course of Storm's history, she battles against the forces of evil. However, during a dark period, she succumbs to the allure of the evil forces in the world. When she loses her powers in a massive supernatural event launched at the mutants, she returns to the life she knew before the X-Men. Her return to Kenya is punctuated by her marriage to T'Challa, the heir to the African kingdom of Wakanda. T'Challa is secretly the superhero Black Panther, and when Storm regains her powers, the pair become a force to be reckoned with in the universe.

The movie adaptations don't depict Storm's full story, however, the transition to the big screen maintains the integrity of the character. She is courageous almost to a fault: she goes into battle knowing she has superior strength, yet doesn't hesitate to expose herself to real bodily danger. Storm is one of the most powerful mutants, but she isn't invincible. When she summons the kind of electrical storm she needs in order to save her X-Men team, she places herself in harm's way. She is an effective warrior who is deeply conscious that her power, if abused, can have devastating consequences for humanity. Her commitment to the common good and the defense of humankind drives her actions. It is fortitude that leads her to sacrifice herself for the good of humanity.

A CHARACTER FOR OUR TIME

From a historical perspective, Storm's inclusion in the fictional Marvel Universe complements many of the pioneering efforts of African Americans in the 1960s and 1970s. Marvel Comics and DC Comics released black male superheroes in 1966 and 1971 respectively, but almost a decade later, Storm emerged as the first black female character. She remains one of the most popular characters in the franchise, including a ranking in *Wizard* magazine as one of the top 100 characters in comics and a ranking by Marvel.com as the third-greatest X-Man. The article from Marvel.com also recognizes Storm's importance in the genre: "One of the strongest female and strongest black characters not just in the history of the X-Men but in all comics, Storm's outer beauty and inner nobility have always transcended gender and race and contributed to her tremendous popularity."[2]

Storm champions social causes, as evidenced by her commitment to the mutant cause. Marvel.com's assessment that Storm transcends both gender and race to become a favorite among male as well as female audiences speaks to the good writing and risks taken in the development of the character. But it also speaks to an audience eager to see black women portrayed authentically as complex characters. That Storm is of black African descent is meaningful because that is part of her identity, but not the all of who she is: "I am a woman, a mutant, a thief, an X-Man, a lover, a wife, a queen. I am all these things. I am Storm, and for me, there are no limits."[3]

These are the kinds of comic book heroines that resonate with me—characters with authenticity. I am, like Storm, a complex woman: a wife, a mother, a sinner, a lover, a teacher, and one day, with the grace of God, a saint. To embrace all the roles she plays, roles that don't limit her but rather make her richer, more complex, and more capable of doing extraordinary things "in the pursuit of the good"—that takes fortitude.

WIFE, QUEEN, AND EMPRESS

When I was in the fifth grade, my classmates were preparing for the sacrament of Confirmation. I had been confirmed as an infant during a turbulent time of religious persecution in Cuba. Many priests had been sent away or left Cuba in fear. The resulting scarcity of priests left a lot of uncertainty for the faithful, and any opportunity for the sacraments was welcomed.

Thus, I found myself sitting quietly in confirmation classes with nowhere to go and unable to participate in the rehearsals and practice. It's a good thing I liked to read, so I took advantage of all the books Sister brought to class. There was volume after volume with stories of saints. Saints who fought in great battles, such as St. Joan of Arc. Saints who fought dragons, such as St. Margaret of Antioch. Saints who did extraordinary things like come back from the dead and fly out of church windows, as St. Christina the Astonishing was purported to have done.

I loved reading adventure stories and science fiction epics, but this collection of saints captured my interest. It was the beginning of my fascination with heroic historical figures. After all, you can create a comic book superhero and give that character whatever attributes you want. But the saints in these books, wow! They were real people doing the unexpected. The common denominator among these saints was their selfless dedication to the poor and marginalized in society. Even at ten years old I understood that this was something important, a deep and beautiful part of living our faith that the saints demonstrated so lovingly.

I also had a bit of a quirky sense of humor and looked for the strangest cases among the saints, so I was drawn away from the mainstream saints in search of the odd or the unusual. When my friends were picking up books that featured St. Patrick or St. Thérèse of Lisieux, I was eyeing the collection that featured St. Cunegunde of Luxembourg. That saint had a great name! I didn't know if it was a man or a woman, but with a great name like that, I was sure going to find out.

I loved history, too, and one of my favorite things to do was color the maps of the Holy Roman Empire. It was then that I fell in love with kings and courts and the tradition of chivalry among knights. St. Cunegunde's life, captured in a tapestry on one of the pages, caught my attention, and I was enthralled.

First, let me clarify that St. Cunegunde was a woman. She was born in about AD 975 and died on March 3, 1040. She was born into a royal line, and one of her ancestors was King Charlemagne, the first Holy Roman emperor. It seems that Cunegunde was destined to be queen and empress. But first, she had to become a wife. In 999, she married Duke Henry of Bavaria, who went on to become the king of Germany in 1002, making Cunegunde his consort and queen. By the year 1014, Henry had been crowned emperor of the Holy Roman Empire, and Cunegunde his empress. That's quite an impressive series of events. Henry II would go on to rule for another decade, dying in 1024 and leaving his queen and empress to finish the work they had begun together.

Their story is filled with mystery and unanswered questions, but it is evident they both led lives of virtue and holiness, as both Cunegunde and Henry II were canonized saints. It's a testament to the power of a sacramental marriage when both spouses work lovingly to help the other get to heaven. It's certain that they led lives of holiness on earth.

Legend tells us that Cunegunde and Henry lived a chaste marriage, and in fact, they had no children. The legend is inspired by claims that Cunegunde wanted to be a nun but accepted marriage without consummation. Henry, too, may have been destined for the life of a religious had circumstances surrounding his cousin's death not placed him in a position to ascend to the throne. Reputedly, Henry used his civil power to order the Abbot of Verdun to accept him as a monk at the Benedictine monastery. In response, the abbot insisted on Henry's obedience as the Rule demanded and sent him back into the world to finish conducting the work of a ruler. Whether or not the story is true, it is indeed known that Henry was a Benedictine oblate. Nevertheless, the couple's fidelity to one another became a point of contention in the court after Henry was crowned emperor.

Henry's reign as king of Germany was marked by numerous wars and skirmishes. In addition, he gifted many lands to dioceses and supported the work of the Church in his kingdom. Cunegunde, as his queen and empress, exercised a great deal of influence in his affairs. She actively participated in his imperial councils, and her support was instrumental in the building of churches and monasteries. She once suffered a grave illness, and, being near death, promised to build a monastery if she recovered. She was true to her word, building the monastery at Kassel.

All these good works, however, became sources of discontent with some of the courtiers, who were at odds with
the king over missed appointments and allegiances. They
accused Queen Cunegunde of treason by illicit liaisons with
a number of men. These accusers may have planted seeds of
doubt in King Henry, who became devastated by the accusa-
tions. However, Queen Cunegunde came forward and made
her case publicly, that she would trust in the Lord to keep
her safe in her innocence of the charges brought against her.
To prove this, and to demonstrate her utter and complete
trust in the Lord, she walked across burning ploughshares,
unmarked. King Henry's joy at seeing her unharmed and
vindicated in the eyes of his detractors caused him to pledge
himself to Queen Cunegunde with renewed fervor.

This scene, captured in tapestry designs and reprinted
in a dusty old book, transfixed me as a child. I was bewil-
dered by the events: that the queen would be accused, that
she would choose to demonstrate her innocence in such a
bizarre and dangerous way, and most of all, that a miracle
occurred and she was unharmed in the demonstration. What
a courageous woman to put her faith so squarely on the line!
This demonstration of the virtue of fortitude surpasses what
we might call mere courage. Cunegunde remained firm in
her denial of adultery, putting her trust in the Lord. Through
fortitude, she was able to face her accusers and overcome
her fears. After all, she walked on hot irons! Where did she
get such strength? Fortitude.

The impact of those adventures, though, did influence
the kinds of stories I loved to read about courtiers and
knights and the royal courts of Europe. In college, I majored
in literature, and took many courses on the Arthurian legends. One course included the importance of courtly influences in the architecture of some cathedrals in Germany,

including a famous statue of a knight on horseback and a beautiful wood triptych. I found the topic interesting, but I was more concerned with the literary tales. Like my study of St. Cunegunde, the information got squirreled away in a corner of my brain.

A few years later I got married and accompanied my husband to his military duty station in Bamberg, Germany. Almost as soon as we settled into our apartment, my husband was called on a mission and left for several weeks. Alone and bored, I occupied my days getting to know the city by going on unscripted adventures. One day I found myself in the middle of a cathedral square, and entered the church. I was stunned to see the statue of the horseman from my textbook. Its name, the Bamberger Horseman, came flooding back to me. How could I have missed that? I recognized the wooden triptych in one of the transepts, and then I got a little nervous and excited. Is this the cathedral that has the only pope buried north of the Alps? Yes! Pope Clemens II, who had been bishop of Bamberg. I quickly shifted my attention to the crypt, and that is when I saw the tomb of Heinrich II and his queen. I couldn't read German and didn't process Heinrich as Henry, but I felt drawn to the tomb and to the images carved along its side depicting the life of the monarch.

When I went around to the other side to study the images of the queen, I almost wept with joy. The panels showed the queen walking across burning ploughshares. It was St. Cunegunde! Everything I read back in the fifth grade came rushing back to me. I stared a long time, looking at the images and reflecting on this saint's life. It was the first time I had consciously prayed at the tomb of a saint. My faith had been flickering in those years, tepid and disinterested, but in that moment, the flame came alive for a brief period, perhaps signaling it was still there, patiently waiting for me.

I read more about the work St. Cunegunde had done in the area. The Diocese of Bamberg and the ecclesiastical buildings in the city, including the cathedral, were constructed as a gift to Cunegunde from Henry. Together, Henry and Cunegunde were committed to building churches, providing service to the poor, and advancing monastic reform.

When Henry died in 1024, Cunegunde remained as regent for a brief period of time during which a new emperor was elected, and then she retired to the abbey she had built at Kassel, where she offered up the very last item that she owned: a fragment of the true cross. She entered the monastery impoverished, having given everything she and Henry owned to the poor or the local churches.

Cunegunde had once shown great fortitude in standing up to her accusers and placing her trust in the Lord. Now, at the end of her life, she put her trust in prayer and opened her heart to an interior life that demonstrated a different kind of fortitude, the fortitude to look into her soul and make herself vulnerable to the Lord. She lived out the rest of her days at the monastery in simplicity and humility, and died in 1040. St. Cunegunde was canonized in 1200 by Pope Innocent III, fifty-three years after her husband, St. Henry, was canonized. Her example spoke to me almost eight hundred years later!

Storm and St. Cunegunde were both queens, and both wielded great power. Storm worked to protect humankind from annihilation. Although she exhibited great courage in battle, it was fortitude that saw her through years of battling for the moral good. St. Cunegunde, on the other hand, endured the emotional pain and threat of execution after she was accused of adultery and betrayal of the Crown. She stood her ground firmly, putting her trust in the Lord for a miracle to deliver her. These stories illustrated for me that while courage, in and of itself, is a valuable asset, the virtue of fortitude enables one to bear the difficulties and challenges in life with an eye to moral behavior and salvation.

DEFENDERS
OF FAIRNESS
AND HONOR

HERMIONE GRANGER AND
ST. MARGUERITE D'YOUVILLE

I'm hoping to do some good in the world.

—Hermione Granger, *Harry Potter and
the Deathly Hallows*

Hermione Granger from J. K. Rowling's Harry Potter series reawakened a favorite childhood fantasy I had while growing up. If only I could blink my eyes like the genie from *I Dream of Jeannie* or wiggle my nose like the good witch, Samantha, from *Bewitched!* I'd have my room picked up in no time! Chores would be a thing of the past; I'd have more adventures than I could shake a wand at! But alas, it was only pretend, and I was just a little girl with no magical powers. I discovered Hermione as an adult reader, but I was swept into her world as if I were a child again, letting my imagination run free in her magical universe.

The trio of heroes in Rowling's Harry Potter universe—Harry Potter, Ron Weasley, and Hermione Granger—are all children who attend Hogwarts School of Witchcraft and Wizardry. There, they learn to master the power of magic, harnessing their emotions and disciplining their actions in order to do good. Yet their universe is not without the existence of evil.

Hermione's presence at Hogwarts signifies more than just adding a girl into the storyline. She brings the gift of her feminine virtues to complement the male heroes. Part of the friends' success, in both the short term and long term, depends on their ability to relate to others. Hermione's emphasis on the importance of relationships strengthens this trio of friends, as she often introduces an element of calm and relational skills that help the trio grow.

Hermione's presence at Hogwarts also bridges the magical realm with the human world. Hermione's parents are not magical, and Hermione was raised in the normal human world. Thus her attendance at the wizarding school creates resentment in some parts of the magical world. Although she sometimes encounters bigotry, Hermione is undeterred in her pursuit of the good. Through Hermione, we see our capacity for strength and courage in a world that seems intent on destroying the good within it. She does not back down from a challenge. Hermione's courage is often underplayed, as she is often described only as intelligent and a talented witch, but it is her quiet fortitude, her stalwart commitment to do right, to "do some good in the world"[1] that casts her as a hero.

When the evil wizard Voldemort reveals himself and his intention to take over the world, Hogwarts's headmaster,

Dumbledore, addresses the gravity of the situation, "It is important to fight, and fight again, and keep fighting, for only then can evil be kept at bay, though never quite eradicated."[2] Hermione courageously stands for what is good in the world, ultimately having to face the evil that is intent on destroying everything she knows and values. Hermione displays fortitude in her willingness to put herself in danger. Her perseverance in carrying out Dumbledore's mission to eradicate Voldemort refines this virtue.

Hermione's fortitude comes from the deep bonds of her friendship with Harry and Ron. We're not made to be alone, and when we are with friends, we become stronger, more capable of accomplishing great things. In the end, it is love that saves them and gives them the courage to fight against Voldemort's army of fiends, and the fortitude to see the battle to the end.

The battle intensifies, and when their situation takes a bad turn, Harry gives Ron and Hermione the opportunity to retreat to safety, but Hermione refuses: "No, Harry, *you* listen, we're coming with you. That was decided months ago—years, really."[3] The three friends are in the battle for the long haul. Hermoine cannot entertain the idea of abandoning her friends in the face of danger. They've been through too much already and held steadfast to each other. Small battles against trolls and bullies in their early years together have honed their magical skills and each new and more dangerous encounter with powerful forces of evil cements their personal bond to protect one another and their mission to see the fight to the end, whatever sacrifice that may entail.

Hermione's courage is not bravado. She knows there's a very real possibility of death, and she is afraid of what may come. Fortitude is not the absence of fear but rather the commitment to power through the fear to do what must be done.

THE COURAGE TO FACE EVIL

Hermione demonstrates the strength of her character in supporting Harry, who is the main protagonist, throughout the series. Hermione's decision to stand by her friend in dangerous situations demonstrates her fortitude. After all, it was Hermione who went behind a treacherous teacher's back and defied orders so she could learn practical defenses against the Dark Arts. This departure from Hermione's usual absolute adherence to the rules is significant. Each edict from that teacher proved to be more and more absurd and unreasonable, and while Hermione liked order and rules, she was more committed to the principles behind them. This act of principled defiance led to the creation of a training ground for many students who would one day need to put into action the defense skills they learned there. Hermione further demonstrates this fortitude in her conviction to join Harry on a dangerous search for what could ultimately destroy Voldemort.

There's no question in my mind about Hermione's character when it comes to courageous acts. It's easy to see this courage in such overt acts of bravery as battling fierce enemies. However, sustaining the commitment to do good while facing imminent danger and possible death requires more than courage. It requires conviction.

Hermione demonstrated courage very early in the series, as a little girl traveling alone to Hogwarts for the first time. Hermione is smart and not afraid to use her intellect in front of her new friends. Although Ron immediately calls her bossy when they meet on the train taking them to the school, she uses magic to fix Harry's broken glasses, demonstrating a skill set neither Harry nor Ron have mastered.

Hermione's nonmagical origins prove to be a source of difficulty throughout her time at Hogwarts, largely because of the amount of bullying she receives from school bully Draco Malfoy and his cohorts. Humans with no magical powers are called Muggles, but every once in a while, a Muggle will be born with magical powers. These people are referred to as Muggle-born, but they can also be referred to by a racist term, mudbloods as Hermoine explains: "It means dirty blood. Mudblood's a really foul name for someone who's Muggle-born. Someone with non-magic parents. Someone like me. It's not a term one usually hears in civilized conversation."[4]

Hermione is often called by this pejorative term, but she refuses to back down from her tormentors. In fact, as she matures and gains confidence in her magical abilities, she considers it a badge of honor. She refuses to be ashamed of her heritage, and while she will acknowledge that others attempt to diminish her with these slurs, Hermione stands up to the accusers and owns her heritage proudly.

There's no question that words can wound, especially when they strike close to home in some semblance of truth. After all, Hermione is, in fact, Muggle-born. It doesn't excuse anyone from using ugly language to describe her, but she uses the slur to empower herself and reach out to others later.

SOCIAL JUSTICE AND THE CARE OF MAGICAL CREATURES

An ongoing subplot that arcs through several volumes of the Harry Potter series features the development of Hermione's social conscience. She leads with compassion and sensitivity, characteristics that develop as she matures into a young woman by the series's end but that she struggles with early in the series. She fancies herself the champion of underdogs everywhere, but rather than focus on herself as a heroic savior, she displays a tender regard for the oppressed and the marginalized. She purchases her cat, Crookshanks, because no one else wants him. Hermione looks beyond his unappealing appearance and sees his intelligence—a good match for her.

Hermione's favorite watchdog cause is the treatment of house elves. Her insistence on the dignity of house elves, a much-abused group of indentured servants, often made her the butt of jokes among the class-conscious pure-blood wizards—a cross she bears, sometimes patiently, sometimes defiantly. Nevertheless, Hermione advocates on the elves' behalf, to amused teasing from her friends.

Hermione understands what it's like to be an outsider. She is a human girl with the rare aptitude for magic. Unfortunately, there are those in the magical realm who reject her and others like her, even to the point of discrimination, active sabotage, and hate. It is, in fact, Hermione's background that separates her from the age-old behaviors of the wizards and strengthens her with the courage to stand up to injustice.

I can relate to her because I, too, have sometimes experienced this sense of being "other" or unwanted. I've felt the sting of being the outsider: I'm an immigrant to the United States, a political refugee who emigrated in the mid-1960s because of tensions in communist Cuba. I have compassion for the new waves of immigrants today, and I feel so much empathy for groups of refugees throughout the world who are fleeing their homelands to escape violence and fear. Like Hermione, I have fostered a love for the marginalized because of my personal circumstances.

Other times in my life I've felt the loneliness of being different. It's a part of the human condition we all experience; it doesn't always come in the form of dramatic exile, but it can be subtle, such as being the only woman in a board meeting or the only basketball player among ballerinas. It shouldn't matter to me, but I've been acutely aware of differences.

To see Hermione overcome her own sense of being different and flourishing in an environment that attempts to oppress her inspires me in my own moments of weakness. Hermione shows up to school enthusiastic and hopeful, yet she almost immediately gets called a *mudblood*. Her presence is suspect and unwanted by a vocal minority that sticks to its outdated and downright evil influences.

Perhaps Hermione's position as an outsider magnifies her sensitivity to those creatures whose inherent dignity is abused. Not just the house elves, but just about every creature that Hagrid, the school groundskeeper, rescues and keeps in his cottage on the edge of the campus inspires some kindness from Hermione. At first, her compassion is just a deeply felt concern, but as Hermione grows, both physically and emotionally, into a strong and confident young woman, her activism grows from just talking about the creatures' dignity to actively engaging in interventions to protect the weak and powerless among them.

My favorite scene in the third book of the series, *The Prisoner of Azkaban*, occurs when Hermione punches bully Draco Malfoy in the nose when she learns he's tormenting the hippogriff that attacked him. Malfoy provokes the poor animal into an aggressive response, and because of it, the hippogriff is scheduled for execution. Hermione does what so many fans have wanted to do: deck Malfoy. Of course, responding with violence isn't an admirable virtue, and she knows that: Hermione stood up to his bullying without resorting to violence when it was personal, but she physically lashes out when he bullies the helpless. However satisfying that might have been, Hermione learns that violence in any form must be avoided, as she sees firsthand how easily some wizards use their powers against others.

When I think of my own experiences as a child, I know that I did not have a fully developed sense of ethnicity and of how others might perceive me or even label me. My status as an immigrant wasn't something that my parents' spoke of—not out of shame but because it should have had no bearing on my performance in school, so it wasn't a conversation anyone found relevant. Was I bullied in school because I was an immigrant? A little bit. Did being bullied affect me? A lot. But I was unaware of the subtle ways it affected me. Instead of becoming a bully myself, I became sensitive to bullying in others. I think that's why I identify so closely with Hermione, why I am quick to champion the little guy and cheer for the underdog. As an adult, I support both financially and through volunteerism those organizations that help the poor and marginalized in society. I understand Hermione's appeal: "I'm a mudblood, and proud of it!"[5]

MUDBLOODS AND DRUNKEN NUNS . . . STICKS AND STONES

Taking on a slur and turning it into something positive, like Hermione's rallying cry, never occurred to me. The religious sisters who taught me at Catholic school during those grade-school years, the Grey Nuns of the Sacred Heart, had some experience with name-calling. Their founder, St. Marguerite d'Youville, and the group of women who came together to form a new religious community under her leadership suffered from ugly slurs in the early years of their order.

St. Marguerite d'Youville was born Marie-Marguerite Dufrost de Lajemmerais on October 15, 1701, in Verannes, Quebec. Her family enjoyed considerable standing in the community, but they almost plunged into extreme poverty when Marguerite's father died suddenly when she was just a little girl.

Her great-grandfather intervened in the desperate affairs of the family. Thanks to him, Marguerite was able to go to school, where she studied under the guidance of Ursuline sisters. When Marguerite finished her schooling, she returned home to teach her younger siblings. Now a young woman, she prepared to marry a young man from a well-to-do family. Unfortunately, her mother, long a widow, decided to marry at the same time. The town's social echelon—a bastion of French society—found her mother's marriage to an Irishman scandalous. The match further affected the family when it was believed the man was unscrupulous in his business dealings.

The union affected Marguerite in a crushing way—her fiancé's family canceled the wedding, and Marguerite was, for the second time in her young life, left bereft. Eventually, the scandal surrounding her mother's new husband settled down. The family relocated to Montreal, and there Marguerite pursued marriage with another young man, Francois d'Youville. The young couple married and went to live with Francois's mother in Montreal. Soon after the wedding, Marguerite became pregnant with their first child, a boy who lived only several months. This was the beginning of a string of heartbreaks for Marguerite. They had five more children, but only two boys survived to adulthood.

Marguerite had no loving and doting husband to alleviate her suffering as a mother. Francois was frequently absent, ostensibly tending to the family's trading business, but in reality squandering the family's money on gambling and alcohol. His business success came from bootlegging: illegal sales of alcohol and other goods with the First Nations tribes of Canada.

While pregnant with their sixth child, Marguerite had to bear the death of her thirty-one-year-old husband, who died of an infection. Although Francois had proven to be a cad, Marguerite cared for him with compassion and love. She suffered alone yet again when their infant child died some months later. Diseases such as measles and chicken pox often took the lives of children in the 1700s, and Marguerite knew too well the kind of hardship families faced. Her personal suffering was forming her heart to be filled with empathy and compassion.

Heavily in debt, thanks to her late husband's behavior, and raising two sons alone, Marguerite turned to the sewing skills she had learned as a young woman under the tutelage of the Ursulines in order to provide for her family. She opened a small shop and turned to her local parish for spiritual support. She became a daily communicant.

She increasingly dedicated herself to ministries that served the community's poor, such as mending their clothes. This small act brings an intimate and gentle touch to the poor. These articles of clothes will be worn. It's an intimate way to acknowledge someone's personal needs at a fundamental level. It's clothing the poor, but more than that, it is an act of love. It is an intersection of service with familiarity.

It was a natural next step for Marguerite to begin taking the poor and destitute into her home. Both of her sons had left for the seminary to become priests, so she not only had the desire but also the space in her home to serve. Marguerite invited a close friend to join her and then two others. In

1737, these women came together formally as a consecrated community, and formed the Sisters of Charity of Montreal.

SINS OF THE PAST

Although Marguerite and her new sisters cared for the destitute in their community and performed great acts of love and charity, the sisters suffered a great indignity because of Marguerite's past. Despite a life spent paying off her late husband's debts and now committed to the care of the poor and sick of Montreal, the specter of Francois's debauchery and bootlegging haunted all her endeavors. When the sisters ran errands in town, the townspeople called them "les souers grises." The literal translation means "the grey sisters" but in the local slang, the taunt had a biting edge, meaning "the tipsy sisters" or "the drunken sisters." How that must have stung Marguerite personally! She might have taken the insults to heart, but how much more hurtful must it have been that the insults were aimed at her sisters who had no association with Francois's illegal dealings. To further add injury, the women were accused of actually getting drunk and continuing the business of bootlegging. Sometimes the cruel words were accompanied by rocks thrown at them! When the rumors increased, the women were sometimes denied Communion. Yet this character assassination didn't stop these courageous women. On the contrary, it affirmed their resolve to continue their work for the poorest and neediest in the community. They exhibited great fortitude in enduring persecution while forging ahead in their mission to serve the poor.

COURAGEOUS TRAILBLAZER

Marguerite's decision to consecrate herself to the poor went against social expectations at the time. She should have remarried, or if the religious life were a true calling, she should have joined a convent. That she chose to use what little resources she had to help the poor was suspect. Marguerite did what women of her class rarely did: she acted according to her will. In truth, Marguerite was acting in accordance with God's will and drew strength from that.

Although Marguerite was getting older and suffered from poor health, she took on the challenge of saving the local general hospital that served many of the poor in Montreal. In spite of the financial and administrative disaster that she inherited, Marguerite and her sisters managed to rescue the hospital. When the hospital later burned to ashes, Marguerite gathered herself up and, after giving thanks to God, took on the courageous task of rebuilding it, despite continued financial challenges. Each setback, rather than defeating her, strengthened her fortitude to face the struggles and persevere.

That hospital became the site of one of her biggest battles in the community. In 1750, after years of work to rehabilitate the hospital, a local magistrate attempted to close it and relocate the poor interned there. Outraged, Marguerite gave a noble defense. She faced the local government courageously and persevered until a technicality was discovered in the hospital's charter, preventing the move. She didn't let any authorities, whether civil or Church, stop her work for the poor. In her own suffering she had grown in faith and the belief in God's tender love for every person.

On both a large and small scale, whether building hospitals or mending clothes, Marguerite and her sisters lived up to the local saying that the Grey Nuns will never refuse to help. That's quite a development in a community that used to taunt them as drunken women.

WOMEN OF INFLUENCE

Over time, the women's selfless work for the poor spoke louder than did the insults. Meanwhile, the small community of women grew, and their reach increased. By 1753, the sisters received a legal charter recognizing them officially before the French crown, and in 1755, the bishop of Quebec, Henri-Marie Dubreil de Pontbriand, formally recognized them as the Sisters of Charity of Montreal. They chose as their habit grey dress, a simple acknowledgment of how they were first identified in the Montreal community. They took the sting out of those early years of torment, perhaps acknowledging it as a part of their determination to forge forward.

This first community of religious sisters grew and expanded into other areas. These expansion efforts led to the formation of new congregations, notably, the Grey Nuns of the Cross, who were first established in Ottawa. The Grey Nuns of the Cross in Ottawa continued serving the communities where they resided in health care and education. Marguerite died in 1771 and was beatified in 1959 by St. John XXIII, who called her the Mother of Universal Charity. St. John Paul II canonized her in 1990.

The Grey Nuns of the Sacred Heart, the English-speaking congregation established in Buffalo, New York, in 1921, continued in the tradition of education but never abandoned their roots in health care and attention to the poor. I was blessed to be taught by a group of Grey Nuns of the Sacred Heart in Georgia. Although they are no longer serving in Georgia, their legacy remains in me—they formed my conscience with a deep sensitivity for the poor and marginalized in society.

Both Hermione and St. Marguerite faced personal trials that could have stifled their desire to interact with and intercede for others. Yet both looked beyond their personal circumstances and risked ridicule (and harm!) by committing themselves to the long-term work of helping the marginalized. Their service, with love, changed their the worlds. And they didn't even need a magic wand.

PUTTING FORTITUDE INTO ACTION

We need not think that the gift of fortitude is necessary only on some occasions or in particular situations. This gift must constitute the tenor of our Christian life, in the ordinary daily routine. As I said, we need to be strong every day of our lives, to carry forward our life, our family, our faith. The Apostle Paul said something that will benefit us to hear: "I can do all things in him who strengthens me" (Phil 4:13). When we face daily life, when difficulties arise, let us remember this: "I can do all things in him who strengthens me." The Lord always strengthens us, he never lets strength lack. The Lord does not try us beyond our possibilities. He is always with us. "I can do all things in him who strengthens me."

Dear friends, sometimes we may be tempted to give in to laziness, or worse, to discouragement, especially when faced with the hardships and trials of life. In these cases, let us not lose heart, let us invoke the Holy Spirit so that through the gift of fortitude he may lift our heart and communicate new strength and enthusiasm to our life and to our following of Jesus."

—Pope Francis, General Audience, Wednesday,
May 14, 2014

1. What does "the tenor of our Christian life" mean? What is the "tenor" of *your* life? Do the two intersect? Name one thing you can do today to better align the two.

2. How do you handle discouragement or hardships? Is prayer a part of your coping strategy? Look up an inspirational line from scripture and write it down. Try Psalms 13 or 26, or my favorite, Jeremiah 29:11.

Keep it close by for those times when you need a reminder that Jesus is our source of strength.

3. Have you ever been afraid, truly fearful in a situation or circumstance in your life? Did you find consolation? Where? With whom? Pope Francis suggests that we invoke the Holy Spirit to come to our aid and give us the gift of fortitude in these circumstances. When we cannot pray for ourselves because circumstances overwhelm us, ask a family member or friend for prayer support.

PART IV

★

SEEKING
TEMPERANCE

Now here's a word that conjures up all kinds of ideas about too much drinking and debauchery—and maybe it's not too far off the mark. Temperance is, after all, the virtue behind Prohibition in the United States.

Merriam-Webster defines temperance as "moderation in action, thought, or feeling," "a habitual moderation in the indulgence of the appetites or passions," and finally as "moderation in or abstinence from the use of alcoholic beverages."[1]

There's that reference to too much alcohol again; it is a bad thing for our health and well-being. But really, temperance is about so much more than not drinking. As the first two definitions indicate, it's about exercising self-control in all areas of our lives. *All areas of our lives*:

> *Temperance* is the moral virtue that moderates the attraction of pleasures and provides balance in the use of created goods. It ensures the will's mastery over

instincts and keeps desires within the limits of what
is honorable. The temperate person directs the sensitive appetites toward what is good and maintains a
healthy discretion: "Do not follow your inclination
and strength, walking according to the desires of your
heart." Temperance is often praised in the Old Testament: "Do not follow your base desires, but restrain
your appetites." In the New Testament it is called
"moderation" or "sobriety." We ought "to live sober,
upright, and godly lives in this world." (CCC, 1809)

That means we should exercise temperance in things we
hadn't even considered. Too much Netflix? Check. Too much
time on social media? Check. Letting my emotions get the
best of me? Check.

The heroines in this section, Lt. Nyota Uhura and Katniss Everdeen, certainly used restraint in their lives, as they
both found themselves in dangerous situations that required
control of their instincts in life-and-death situations. St. Kateri Tekakwitha and St. Mary MacKillop also exhibited this
virtue in the way they handled themselves with restraint
and self-control when dealing with people opposed to their
faith and ideals.

CHAMPIONS
OF CARING AND
COMPASSION

KATNISS EVERDEEN AND
ST. MARY MACKILLOP

My spirit. This is a new thought. I'm not sure exactly
what it means, but it suggests I'm a fighter. In a sort
of brave way.

—Katniss Everdeen, *The Hunger Games*

I came to The Hunger Games trilogy during the highly antic-
ipated release of the third book in the series. Both *The Hunger
Games* and *Catching Fire* had been available for some time,
and I noted the frenzy over the imminent launch of the conclusion, *Mockingjay*. Not one to jump on board just because
everyone was reading it, I needed a good reason to pick up
the first book.

"Because you're going to get swept up in the story and fight over my copy of *Mockingjay*." That was all I needed to know from one of my children, a voracious reader with similar tastes in books. She was right.

The protagonist, Katniss Everdeen, instantly became my favorite character in years. She's smart. She's athletic. She's courageous. She's resourceful. She's complex. She kicks ass.

The older I get, the more I want my stories to have a happy ending. I want the girl to get the boy. I want happily-ever-after. It didn't look like The Hunger Games was going to grant that wish, but I liked Katniss right away, and I wanted to know more about what drives her.

The books are set in a future postapocalyptic North America. The continent has been divided into twelve districts that support the Capitol. Katniss lives in the poorest district, a mining center. Her father dies in a mining accident, leaving her mother depressed and incapable of caring for her family. Facing starvation, Katniss becomes the provider for the family at the young age of eleven. She secretly learns to hunt, an illegal activity in the districts, but she becomes an expert archer and hones the survival skills she will later use.

Like so many heroes in literature and film, Katniss is reluctant to play the role of hero, yet the story begins with one of the most heroic acts of love. Katniss volunteers to take her little sister's place in a terrible lottery for the gladiator-style Hunger Games. The Hunger Games are an annual event, run by the Capitol, to remind the districts of their powerlessness against their rulers. She knows her little sister would never survive the brutal battle to the death. Thus, her decision to volunteer immediately gets the attention of the world.

Although I typically avoid postapocalyptic stories because of their grim and dark themes, I found Katniss compelling. She displays strength and courage, coupled with the desire to protect what is good—she wants to protect her sister's innocence and care for her family. I found these traits worth emulating. She lives in a society that has found peace through a tenuous status quo. The Hunger Games is an annual contest, run by the Capitol, to remind the districts of the consequences of rebellion: Every year each district must provide a male and a female contestant for the Hunger Games, where only one contestant can survive, and win. The games, televised to all the districts, ostensibly serve as an outlet for the violent tendencies of humanity. This tribute, in human lives, reminds the masses of what life would be like without the order mandated by the Capitol.

It does not yet occur to Katniss to reject the games as a cruel and brutal practice, and I was drawn to the story precisely because I wanted to see her succeed and later take down this perverse practice. After winning the Hunger Games through cunning and bravery, Katniss believes she is free of the contest. However, the government exploits Katniss and demands she return for a second competition. Katniss begins to rebel against the Capitol, exposing lie after lie as a widespread rebellion sweeps across the districts.

Finally, she enters a third and final game, ostensibly in support of the new government but secretly driven by revenge. In a reversal of the virtue of prudence, Katniss uses her strength in critical thinking to transition from being the hunted to the hunter.

THE HUMAN CONDITION

Many science fiction and fantasy stories take place in other worlds with alien characters that resemble humans but aren't. This literary tradition allows the authors to explore social themes without the stories being technically about our society, which affords the reader an objective view. However, the world created in The Hunger Games is our world, populated by human beings. People like us. We don't have to look further than the ancient Roman Empire to see a precursor to the fictional Hunger Games in the gladiator battles that were fought to the death as a form of entertainment.

The plausibility of this story and the development of Katniss's character through this plausible reality had a different effect on me than some heroines with superpowers or the ability to travel through space and time. I found myself invested in her choices, trying to get inside her head to fully understand what she experienced. In an unexpected way, Katniss became everywoman for me. If she did these things, I wondered, could I? This adventure, more so than others, became a vicarious exploration of the human condition.

Katniss demonstrates great courage early in the story. Although courage is laudable in a battle to the death, I think far more admirable is Katniss's temperance, her ability to moderate her actions according to reason. Katniss doesn't just act in the moment; she thinks carefully about the consequences and chooses according to the best outcome. For the most part, her choices lead to the good.

Katniss displays self-restraint as a girl learning to hunt. Her initial excitement at sighting prey and learning to discipline herself to keep from attempting a poor shot serves her well. She refines her skill, learning to wait for the right moment not only to have a successful shot but also to avoid wasting arrows.

Katniss becomes an excellent markswoman and, thanks to that, feeds her family and sometimes has something left over for trading. This skill also serves Katniss well when she is deeply entrenched in the Hunger Games. Although it is inevitable that she will need to kill or be killed, Katniss actively focuses on survival. As in her hunting days, she hides and observes, looking for the opportune time to act in order to garner the best possible outcome.

Several times during the Games, Katniss demonstrates the self-restraint that saves her from going into dangerous situations that are designed to give a false sense of security. She creates alliances instead. Her decisions for the good outside her own immediate safety not only save her but also save her male counterpart from her district, Peeta. Katniss weighs her choices and makes decisions according to her sense of the world; she doesn't simply accept what the Capitol foists upon her. She thinks of consequences for Peeta, her family, the other contestants, even society as she understands it. Katniss learns to control her impulses, not because she feels more human than the Capitol game-makers but because she realizes how easily she could become an animal, a predator. It unsettles her, as she recognizes that, on some level, she would like to behave like an animal and kill all her oppressors. She chooses not to succumb to those impulses.

DEFIANCE LEADS TO REBELLION

Even though Katniss recognizes she is nothing more than a pawn in the politics of the Hunger Games, she refuses to lower herself and to hold the same disregard for life as her oppressors. When fellow contestant Rue is killed in the game, Katniss covers her body in flowers as a gesture of love and respect. After watching the unfolding of violence before her, she begins to weigh the benefits of rebelling against the traditions of the games, not just for personal gain but to benefit society. By this point, I couldn't put down the first book because I had too many questions: Will she be able to take this defiance to the next level and sacrifice herself for society? Can she conspire to overthrow the Capitol? We see that possibility in the endgame.

Katniss captures the attention of the Capitol with her clever positioning during the game. In the end, Katniss refuses to kill Peeta, and instead plans their simultaneous deaths, an act that forces the Capitol to declare them co-victors. The Capitol finds itself in the position of scrambling to put a spin on the events. The massive broadcast of the games as a measure to control the public has backfired, as all the districts are glued to the events as they unfold. Beaten, the Capitol allows the dual victory, and the seeds of discontent and rebellion have taken root.

In the next book, *Catching Fire*, Katniss matures with the growing awareness of the Capitol's lies. She discovers there are rebellions taking place across the districts, and learns there is a thirteenth district, one the Capitol has been unable to control. Although she sympathizes with the rebels—after all, her suicide pact with Peeta was an act of defiance against the Capitol—she is still fearful for her family's safety and reluctantly cooperates with the Capitol's agenda. By the events of the final book, *Mockingjay*, Katniss accepts her role as the face of the rebellion. She recognizes that her personal victories in the games have inspired rebels everywhere to rise up against the Capitol's totalitarian government. She plays her allegiance carefully, trying to protect those she loves, but in a terrible turn of events, her sister and other children who had been guaranteed refuge are murdered in cold blood.

The murders devastate Katniss and affect her mental health. The massacre gives the rebellion a final boost in motivation to overthrow the government, and they capture the Capitol and arrest President Snow. Katniss, as the hero of the rebellion, is called upon to publicly execute President Snow for his crimes. However, Katniss learns that the massacre was a ploy developed by the rebellion's leader to inspire a final battle to victory. In a stunning move, Katniss spares Snow and instead assassinates the new president, the rebellion's leader.

I don't like this development in the story. Prior to taking justice into her own hands, Katniss has displayed strength of character and commitment to the good. Katniss develops the virtue of temperance over time. As a child learning to hunt, she laid a foundation for discipline that saves her life in the games. Although I've never been hunting with a bow and arrow like Katniss, I do accompany my husband when he goes fishing. I'm not very good at it. The moment I feel even the slightest nibble on my line I get excited and immediately pull up on my rod. I lose the fish every time. My impulsivity and lack of self-control keeps me from enjoying the thrill of catching a fish. I should remember Katniss the next time I'm out on the fishing pier.

Katniss hones her self-control in the forest as a hunter, and successfully applies this virtue in other areas of her life, especially with the demands of being a contestant for her district. It's important to note that as long as love motivates Katniss, the exercise of temperance, while not easy, yields positive results. In fact, almost all the results point to the good. She survives in the Games, she treats the other contestants with dignity, and she saves Peeta's life.

Her strong independence and resourcefulness have kept her alive and kept the rebellion strong. The early days of hunting for survival, the life and death drama of the Hunger Games, and finally, the strategic demands of leading a rebellion have all been cause for suffering, but she has always weighed the risks and chosen the right path. Until now.

HOPELESS, LOST, AND FOUND

Katniss may be a survivor, but she lacks hope. Her success in the Games brings her fame, but somewhere in the arena she loses her motivation. Once upon a time, she was killing animals to provide for her family. Then, she had to use those skills for her own survival. Now, her hunting skills had turned into something else, something dangerous.

Every move is a calculation. Those early years taught her to assess risk and take risks only when the outcome had the potential for success. Because of that, she has no room in her life for romance or any other relationships. She doesn't believe her relationships could be successful. Her father dies, her mother loses her mind to grief, her little sister is murdered. There is no love in her future, only survival.

Nevertheless, Katniss knows right from wrong. She pursues the good in deplorable conditions: hunting to feed her family even though it is illegal, sacrificing her life to save her sister, choosing survival in the Hunger Games rather than actively hunting other contestants. Katniss makes decisions based on the good they will produce. It's a sign of a strong moral compass, and it shows her temperance. That's why I was disappointed when she assassinated the new president.

Yet Katniss behaves consistently, even in this act of murder. From the very beginning, she identifies herself as a hunter. She kills out of necessity and never for sport. Because survival is her motivation, she questions her place in a new world where she doesn't have to worry about hunting for food. Katniss is most comfortable as a hunter. In that regard, her final act is an act of protection for the new order. That she intended to kill herself immediately after this speaks to a decision that must have tormented her. After all, Katniss already demonstrated in the games that she abhorred killing, even for survival. She's deemed mentally unfit and is not prosecuted, but I think she was, in fact, quite clear-headed.

This is why I dislike dystopian stories. Katniss fails me. She fails herself. This isn't the happy ending where she goes off into the sunset with her true love. And there's no redemption in her final act. I can't accept this lack of redemption or claim that Katniss is a good role model, specifically because she fails when it counts the most.

Instead, we get a messy ending—a character who suffered a great deal and continues to suffer. Katniss commits murder in cold blood, not in a moment of passion or self-defense. I'm disappointed and dismayed by how easily she comes to this decision because it is plausible. After a lifetime of careful restraint, Katniss gives up and gives in to her instinct for revenge. It reminds me of how perilously close to sin I am at every moment. It reminds me that however much I may practice and attempt to perfect virtue, without God's grace, I am weak and prone to fail.

If the story were to end here, my disappointment would remain, but we are given a glimpse into her life after the fall of the Capitol. The epilogue takes us into the future, where Katniss has returned to her childhood home. She settles down with Peeta and starts a family. But it isn't an easy peace for Katniss. She continues to be plagued by nightmares and memories, filled perhaps with regrets if not remorse. Yet she chose to leave the fighting for Peeta and a chance at peace. Once hopeless, she chooses hope in a new generation and says yes to life, yes to a growing family of her own.

BEFRIENDING A SAINT

Katniss affected me in unexpected ways because I wanted to like her; I wanted to say, *Here's a character that encompasses*

all the virtues I want to emulate. It didn't work out that way
for me. Still, she had me reflecting on her motives and the
choices she made, and that's what good literature does.
Good literature should prod us a little and provide opportunities for reflections about ourselves, our values, the things
we can learn from these fictional characters.

St. Mary MacKillop's story prodded me a little, too.
She touched me because of her humility and suffering and
affected me deeply not as a fictional literary figure but as a
real, holy woman of God. The difference is, of course, that
she's a true role model, a saint who invited me to get to know
her better during an unexpected encounter with her shrine
while I was on vacation in Scotland. I had already been reading about St. Mary MacKillop, still unsure of her inclusion in
this book, when I recognized the name of her father's birthplace in Roybridge, near Inverness. My husband and I were
looking for a Catholic church, and we found St. Margaret's,
the site of Mary's own pilgrimage to her family's origins.
Praying at the little shrine opened my heart to Mary's heroic
patience and humility, which had helped her discern the
best way to serve the poor and marginalized in the face of
opposition from clergy who wanted administrative control
of her new religious order and their schools. I knew then I
needed to share her story here.

Mary shares some things in common with Katniss Everdeen, but her actions had different results, which I found
intriguing. Where struggle and disappointment limited Katniss's ability to love, they magnified love in Mary. Where the
fictional Katniss ultimately failed to inspire, the saintly Mary
used her cleverness for good. Mary's story is a complicated
one that features excommunication—and redemption—and
I was intrigued.

Mary MacKillop, Australia's first saint, was born on January 15, 1842, in Fitzroy, Victoria, close to Melbourne. She was the oldest of eight children born to Scottish immigrants. Mary's parents met in Australia although they were both born in Scotland and from the same area. Australia was still very much a new frontier in the mid-1800s and had the allure of opportunity. Her father, Alexander, arrived first to seek his fortune in this new land. He had studied for the priesthood and spent years at the seminary in Rome before returning to Scotland to finish his studies. He dropped out right before his ordination and sought a new life in Australia. Her mother, Flora, arrived in Australia a few years after Alexander. They met through his kindness in helping Flora's family get settled; within months they were married.

Although a highly educated man and devoted to his family, Alexander was a terrible businessman who failed at just about everything he attempted and even spent a period of almost two years abroad in Scotland, leaving the family to fend for themselves. These failures, of course, affected the family, but in spite of his inability to provide for his family, Alexander put to good use his academic training and educated his eight children in both classical and religious studies. Their education would serve the children well as adults, but in their moment of need, it was young Mary who rose to the occasion and became the principle provider for the family.

The MacKillops suffered devastating poverty as the children were growing up, and they all had to contribute what they could to the family. Mary, especially, felt a great responsibility to her siblings. By the time she was fourteen years old, Mary was working full time to provide for the household. Like the fictional Katniss, Mary's first choices in life were to support the ones she loved. Several years later she took a job as a governess, which gave her a more dependable income.

Her job not only opened Mary to the possibility of earning a good living, but it also opened her heart in another direction. She felt committed to helping others get out of poverty the way she did: by learning the basic life skills that would help them fend for themselves. In 1860, Mary starting offering lessons to the local poor children, teaching them how to do basic math and write letters, to keep records and to read the *Catechism*. This practical approach to education caught the interest of the local priest, Fr. Julian Woods, who found in Mary a kindred spirit.

Mary had longed for the religious life but could not see a fit for herself, given the responsibilities she had assumed to care for her family. Fr. Woods had seen the deep need to provide a Catholic education to the children in Australia, and he prayed for a uniquely Australian order of nuns who understood the cultural needs of the poor in the countryside and would be able to not only serve the poor but also live among them. Mary immediately embraced the idea even though her mother was opposed to it. In 1866, the Sisters of St. Joseph of the Sacred Heart were established, and Mary became Sr. Mary of the Cross and the first superior of the order.

Sr. Mary didn't rush into anything, but when she had carefully discerned a direction, she moved with deliberate action. When Fr. Woods established the first Catholic school in Penola later that year, Mary and her sisters, dressed in their postulant habits, reported for work at the school, sending a powerful message to those in the community (and her family) that this was the direction she intended for her life.

The school was a success, and so was the order, which grew rapidly in those early days. The sisters' model of teaching the poor in the rural areas of the Australian bush soon caught the attention of Bishop James Quinn in Brisbane. Sr. Mary and some of her sisters were invited to Brisbane to build schools there. Unfortunately, this project was difficult for the sisters because their order was misunderstood. The nuns lived in the community, learning the ways of the people they served, instead of living in convents. This was a departure from the way the clergy understood religious sisters, and it caused some power struggles between the bishop, who demanded obedience, and Sr. Mary, who tried to maintain autonomy for the order. The young superior learned much about leadership and Church affairs in Australia during that year.

By 1871, there were more than 120 women in the thriving order, and Sr. Mary endeavored to have personal contact with each sister. She took their welfare and her position as mother quite seriously. When she returned to Adelaide, where the Sisters of St. Joseph of the Sacred Heart were established, she discovered more rumblings of difficulty. Bishop Quinn recommended that the sisters change their Rule, place themselves under the diocesan authority, and move to convents. Sr. Mary resisted and sent an appeal to Bishop Laurence Sheil of Adelaide, in which she carefully explained her position. Sadly, this letter led to greater misunderstanding. Bishop Sheil, believing Sr. Mary was being disobedient and insubordinate, excommunicated her.

What a stunning turn of events! Sr. Mary accepted the excommunication calmly, turning to God with the security that he knew her heart. But the excommunication was hurtful, of course, and caused untold difficulties, as contact with Mary would lead to other excommunications. Dozens of sisters left the order in solidarity, and Mary withdrew to the kindness of a Jewish family that housed her during this dark time.

Some months later, the excommunication was reversed. Bishop Sheil was on his deathbed and sent word that he had a change of heart, but the damage to her reputation was done. Once the excommunication was lifted, though, Mary went to Rome to petition for a formal approval of the order's Rule in order to avoid further debate over the group's autonomy. She met with Pope Pius IX, hoping to have his support for the Rule. Pope Pius knew of her and even referred to her as "the excommunicated one," but she felt his pastoral presence as a loving father. He pledged her his support.

During the long wait before the ratification of the Rule, Sr. Mary traveled throughout Europe, including a trip to Scotland to visit her parents' birthplace. It must have been difficult to learn about her roots while waiting on the mercy of others to determine her future. I hope the beauty and serenity of Roybridge gave her some consolation.

When she returned to Australia, Sr. Mary's troubles continued as another bishop opened an investigation of the sisters' order in Adelaide. The investigation yielded no irregularities; nevertheless, Sr. Mary was removed from her duties immediately, with no explanation, and sent to Sydney. The archbishop in Sydney, Patrick Francis Moran, received her enthusiastically. Archbishop Moran, it turns out, was appointed by Rome to look into the complaints against Sr. Mary. The diocesan fight to gain control of the religious order continued, but Rome decreed that a Mother General of the Sisters of St. Joseph of the Sacred Heart, not a bishop, would continue to run the Rule of the order. However, Sr. Mary was removed from her position of leadership and Sr. Barnard was appointed Mother General. Sr. Barnard served as Mother General until her death ten years later. At that time, a new election was held and Sr. Mary once again took the leadership of the order until her death.

At the time of Sr. Mary's death, almost 800 women had joined the Sisters of St. Joseph of the Sacred Heart; 117 schools operated throughout Australia and New Zealand, serving more than 12,000 children. In spite of administrative challenges over autonomy, Sr. Mary's brief period of excommunication, and the later reassignment of the order's Mother General, the sisters flourished in their work. Sr. Mary's last words to her sisters, in a letter, encapsulate what she lived: "Whatever troubles may be before you, accept them cheerfully, remembering whom you are trying to follow. Do not be afraid. Love one another, bear with one another, and let charity guide you in all your life."[1]

Sr. Mary's final words to her sisters encompassed the temperance she had displayed her whole life. From the time of her youth, Mary worked diligently to support her family instead of lashing out angrily at the injustice of having to go to work as a child. As the Mother General of her order, she maintained a steady advocacy for the integrity of the Rule and the sisters' mission with the poor. Even, perhaps *especially*, during her excommunication, Sr. Mary displayed a calm self-control so as not to escalate tensions.

When called to a moment of crisis, the fictional Katniss threw in her lot with the mindset of her oppressors, exacting her own tribute for her sister's death. St. Mary MacKillop practiced temperance at every opportunity, and through God's grace fostered love in the face of adversity.

EXPLORERS OF
PEACE AND FAITH

LT. NYOTA UHURA AND
ST. KATERI TEKAKWITHA

Hailing frequencies open, sir.

—Lt. Uhura, *Star Trek*

I've been a lifelong fan of the Star Trek franchise, so I've saved for last my favorite heroine, Lt. Nyota Uhura.

When I was a very little girl watching *Star Trek* for the first time with my father, I thought Lt. Uhura was very pretty. I didn't understand that she was the only woman working on the bridge of the *Enterprise* or even that this character and this role for Nichelle Nichols challenged society's views of women and people of color in the 1960s. I was just a kid enjoying a story. When I played with my friends, I never pretended to be the captain; I wanted to look at the computers and monitors and listen to things just like Lt. Uhura!

When I re-watched the series in the early 1970s, I was just becoming a teenager and could articulate reasons for my admiration. I understood the importance of having a woman, and especially an African American actor, playing a non-stereotypical role in a prime-time television show. Actor Nichelle Nichols has revealed that she had decided to quit the series after its first season to pursue a career on Broadway, but Dr. Martin Luther King Jr., who was a fan of the show, encouraged her to stay in order to serve as a role model:

> He said, "You cannot," and so help me this man practically repeated verbatim what Gene [Roddenberry, the show's creator] said. He said, "Don't you see what this man is doing, who has written this? This is the future. He has established us as we should be seen. Three hundred years from now we are here. We are marching, and this is the first step. When we see you, we see ourselves, and we see ourselves as intelligent and beautiful and proud." He goes on and I'm looking at him and my knees are buckling. I said, "I . . . , I . . ." And he said, "You turn on your television and the news comes on and you see us marching and peaceful, you see the peaceful civil disobedience, and you see the dogs and see the fire hoses, and we all know they cannot destroy us because we are there in the twenty-third century.[1]

Nichols put her desire to pursue a musical career on hold and considered Dr. King's words. She could have moved forward in her stage career, but instead exhibited the same temperance, the same disciplined ability "toward what is good" that Lt. Uhura displays. Nichols stayed on for the run of the series and then voiced her character in the animated series and in video games. She also continued her role as Uhura for six movies.

In 1979, when *Star Trek: The Motion Picture* was released, I was ready to embrace Star Trek as a young adult with growing sensibilities of the social justice themes traditionally explored by the series. The plot of the movie wasn't great, but watching it was like being reunited with friends. Capt. Kirk, Mr. Spock, Dr. McCoy . . . it was great to see them, but when I saw Lt. Uhura still wearing that communication device in her ear, I knew I was home with my old pals.

SENSITIVITY IN COMMUNICATIONS

Star Trek gave its audience new ways to look at things, and its strength was in its crew. It's difficult to talk about Lt. Uhura in isolation because she was an important part of the collective action on the bridge of the *Enterprise*. Of course, Capt. Kirk and Mr. Spock dominated the stories, but I always felt that Lt. Uhura, even though she wasn't a major player, consistently contributed to the missions' success.

In *Star Trek: The Original Series*, Uhura serves aboard the USS *Enterprise* as the head communications officer. She specializes in linguistics and communications but has expertise in a number of other scientific areas, including philology, which is the study of language—not just the grammatical structures but also the historical and social elements. This specialty enhances her ability to bring cultural sensitivity to her language analysis, especially when the crew encounters interstellar cultures while on diplomatic missions. In addition to establishing direct communications from the bridge to the crew, Uhura also monitors transmissions in space that include signals for help and, sometimes, secret or coded communications from hostile alien races. She demonstrates resilience and creativity, often rewiring her own console in order to establish necessary connections.

Uhura's presence on the bridge also indicates that she is likely in the line of command in case an emergency requires that someone take over Capt. Kirk's leadership of the *Enterprise*. She has, on occasion, taken the helm or navigation of the ship, so we know she has the skills to maneuver the ship.

Kirk recognizes Uhura's skills. Her ability to step into a battle situation and still be aware of her communications responsibilities isn't just about multitasking. She understands that all the elements of the bridge are interrelated and necessary for success. This is where Uhura's personality shines. She is steady and cool, able to assess information and act accordingly. She demonstrates a great deal of temperance in a position where tensions can run high, especially in the heat of battle.

Experience tempers Uhura's confidence in her abilities, especially if she disagrees with an order. We see a calm and cool Uhura execute her orders. But she's also human and loses her cool a time or two. It's important for me to see this touch in a character; it makes her not just human but also someone I can relate to. In the episode "The Naked Time," the crew of the *Enterprise* gets infected by a space germ that causes their inhibitions to fall away. One manic behavior leads to another. In one scene, a crew member locks himself away with access to the ship's intercom, singing nonstop love songs to the crew and carrying on an obnoxious, incessant chatter:

> *Kirk:* [*stalking over to a frantically working Uhura*] At least *try* cutting him off!
> *Uhura:* [*shouting*] Sir, if I could cut him off, don't you think I—? [*She suddenly remembers to whom she's speaking and visibly gets her temper under control.*] Yes, sir. I'll keep trying.
> *Kirk:* [*ruefully*] Sorry.

[*Uhura smiles back at him and gets back to work.*]

At this point in the action, everyone on the bridge is on edge, including the captain. In this exchange, Uhura masters her instinct to respond angrily. She starts to mouth off at the captain over the obvious: she is, in fact, trying to cut off the transmission. That she corrects herself mid-outburst demonstrates her willingness to work on temperance. Uhura's example shows me that we are works in progress. I tend to be a little mouthy sometimes. It got me into trouble as a teenager and young adult until I learned that this virtue demands ongoing attention from me. I still struggle with it today. Apparently, so does Uhura.

One of the things I enjoy about Lt. Uhura's self-confidence is her ability to take care of herself. Temperance doesn't require us to be submissive and patiently bear everything. In that same episode, she encounters an infected crew member, Mr. Sulu, who grabs her in a swashbuckling fugue. Her response to his unwanted overtures makes me laugh every time:

Sulu: I'll rescue you, fair maiden!
Uhura: [*deadpan*] Sorry, neither.

Uhura doesn't need to be rescued, and her self-awareness regarding the double meaning of "fair" is just plain funny. Throughout the episode, she is an integral part of a team racing against time to solve the problem of the epidemic, and a cool and calm steadiness must prevail in the face of panic.

Uhura is all business when she's on the bridge.

In the episode "Who Mourns for Adonais?" Mr. Spock needs Lt. Uhura to rewire the communications system. The *Enterprise* has been incommunicado because of a system breakdown, and concerns for the safety of the away team, including the captain, worry Spock. Lt. Uhura's response to Spock, while respectful, has an edge that shows both her respect for his authority and her professionalism and self-control.

> *Uhura:* I'm connecting the bypass circuit now, sir. It should take another half hour.
> *Spock:* Speed is essential, Lieutenant.
> *Uhura:* Mr. Spock, I haven't done anything like this in years. If it isn't done just right, I could blow the entire communications system. It's very delicate work, sir.
> *Spock:* I can think of no one better equipped to handle it, Ms. Uhura. Please proceed.

I would feel micromanaged in this situation, but Uhura embraces temperance and maintains her composure, even with Spock looking over her shoulder as she works in tight quarters.

While Uhura is all business on the bridge, off-duty she enjoys herself and is well-liked by her colleagues. She's known to sing in the crew's recreation room, and enjoys a friendly relationship with Spock. When Spock plays the Vulcan lyre, she accompanies him. Sometimes it leads to teasing. In the episode "Charlie X," Uhura and Spock perform a song for the crew in the lounge that implies Spock is irresistible to the women onboard the *Enterprise*; Uhura enjoys a playful performance trying to get Mr. Spock to react.

Although he remains impassive, Uhura's laughter and comfortable demeanor around him shows a level of friendly intimacy we don't see on the bridge. Mastery over desires and instincts isn't about turning ourselves into unfeeling robots, but rather, ordering our behavior so it is appropriate to our circumstances. I love that Lt. Uhura displays steady control on the bridge and warmth and laughter in her social interactions.

I've always felt Lt. Uhura's standout moment occurred in the serious episode titled "Bread and Circuses" because of the respect she both gives and receives in her interactions with the bridge crew, especially the captain. The crew is confused by an alien society that persecutes sun worshipers. These sun worshipers practice a religion of love and brotherhood, and it confounds the crew that these peaceful people are imprisoned and executed. Lt. Uhura, who has been listening to their broadcasts, realizes what is actually happening: "I'm afraid you have it all wrong, all of you," she says. "I've been monitoring some of their old-style radio waves, the empire spokesman trying to ridicule their religion, but he couldn't. Well, don't you understand? It's not the sun up in the sky. It's the Son of God."[2] Lt. Uhura tells superior officers that they are wrong. She does this respectfully, and with the confidence of someone who knows she is respected and will be heard. This scene demonstrates to me the value of temperance in relationships. Because she isn't given to inappropriate outbursts every time she disagrees with an order, her chain of command listens to her now.

Gene Roddenberry, the show's creator and producer, strove to develop a show that had a humanist approach, so to have religion so overtly a part of the episode was an extraordinary move—Uhura spoke up and corrected her superior officers with extraordinary news. She did this with tact and a matter-of-fact delivery that exemplified her professionalism throughout the series. I wish I had put her example into practice in more than one meeting over the course of my career in education!

Nichelle Nichols's portrayal of Lt. Nyota Uhura begins with the character's first posting in Starfleet and encompasses her entire career; in spite of limited screen time during the series, Uhura develops as a three-dimensional character. I admire her control in all areas of her job, from managing communications to maintaining the technology to, the most difficult, interpreting the cultural nuances in language to help the captain in his diplomatic duties.

REBOOTING A FRANCHISE

When I first heard that director J. J. Abrams was working on a reboot of *Star Trek*, I was equal parts elated and apprehensive. I knew that Abrams would produce something out of this world, literally! But I also didn't want him to mess with the characters and stories I'd come to love over the fifty years of Star Trek history. I've enjoyed all the spin-offs of the original series, seen all the movies, and even read dozens and dozens of authorized novels. Once upon a time, I might have even written some fan fiction—maybe.

As a fan, I was uneasy about a reboot.

One part of my apprehension about a *Star Trek* reboot had a lot to do with how the new actors would interpret these beloved characters. When I think of Uhura, I think of Nichelle Nichols's characterization. Another part of it was in not wanting anyone to change the canon. I liked things just the way they were. I didn't want to be challenged to leave my comfort zone.

Any misgivings I had were eliminated when I saw the first movie trailer. Wow! I was reminded of my anticipation when *Star Trek: The Motion Picture* was released in 1979. I got over my trepidation immediately and watched Abrams's *Star Trek* on opening weekend in 2009.

A time-travel script reconciled the canon issue by creating a timeline change. Although it can be a cheap and easy way to tell new stories with established characters, it worked in the Star Trek universe. With these changes, I recognized that I was being pushed a little outside my comfort zone, but that's exactly what *Star Trek* did in the 1960s. The original series excelled at telling stories, so I would have to give these new stories a chance. I was also determined to be open to actor Zoe Saldana's interpretation of Uhura. I wasn't disappointed.

FLASHBACK TO THE BEGINNING

Abrams's reboot delivers a visual punch that none of the previous Star Trek films have achieved. Visual effects keep getting better, and this film has stunning effects and gorgeous vistas. The opening car chase left me breathless and established young James T. Kirk as a maverick. Later, when Kirk and Uhura meet in a bar, Kirk's unwanted overtures annoy Uhura. He persists, and she deflects, but Kirk's inability, or rather, unwillingness to stand down from his bravado gets him beat up by Uhura's companions.

I didn't get the feeling Uhura needed rescuing, but we see signs of her restraint when dealing with Kirk. She matures throughout this first film and the films that follow to fully develop this character trait.

It's important to note that *this* Uhura, Saldana's interpretation, is a younger woman. She is still a cadet at Starfleet Academy. I enjoy seeing this young version of the character and learning more about her background. It's especially gratifying to see more of Uhura's personal life in this introductory film. We see her in her dorm room frustrated by her roommate. We also learn she is a serious student, which explains why the older Uhura is such an accomplished expert in various fields. Although the reboot sets events into a different universe, the characters are fundamentally the same.

And because it's a parallel universe, we finally learn Uhura's first name. In a running gag between Uhura and Kirk, his attempts at getting her name are shot down repeatedly. The longtime fans in the audience empathize with Kirk; we want to know her name, too! Uhura's first name was never mentioned in the original series, and therefore never became a part of the canon until now. The omission was not intentional, but fans have always been curious about the name. Finally, Kirk overhears it in the turbolift.

> Spock: [*standing across from Lt. Uhura before he and Kirk are about to be beamed onto a Romulan warship*] I will be back.
> Uhura: [*leaning in*] You better be! I'll be monitoring your frequency.
> Spock: [*actually quite emotional*] Thank you, Nyota.
> Kirk: [*after Uhura leaves*] So her first name's Nyota?
> Spock: I have no comment on the matter.

This sets up a couple of important things about Uhura. First, she has no respect for Kirk. His brashness in their first meeting and subsequent disregard for authority at the Academy make him an obnoxious annoyance. She won't give him power over her by revealing her name.

And then he becomes her captain.

Uhura's first exchange with Kirk on the bridge of the *Enterprise* acknowledges his position, but she can't help herself from saying "Captain," with a sarcastic bite. The young Uhura struggles with self-control. She's passionate and quick to state her mind with no tact. In many ways she's a match for Kirk. While this is a departure from the way we see the mature Uhura, Nichelle Nichols, after a meeting with Zoe

Saldana, had insight into how these two interpretations of the character are reconciled:

> Zoe played it just like I was saying, a young recruit. They're having fun. It's exciting. They're serious about their training, but when they're off duty they're like young people. . . . I said, "I created her as a serious person, but not that serious." I told her that Uhura was as serious as cancer when we were on duty, but that when we were off duty she could be in the rec room singing and teasing Spock with that song about him. . . . When [the movie] was over I understood what [Zoe] was talking about when she said, "I wish I had spoken to you before I started," because she was playing it light and flirty at the beginning. The time [during filming when] I spoke to her was the time they were then going on the ship. Do you remember the scene where she says, "No, I'm going! I was promised this, and I'm going," and they had to take her on? She was destined to go on. She kissed Spock in a different way and said, "I'll see you on board." When she walked on board she was a full-blown Uhura in every manner and the way that I had created the character.[3]

Capt. Kirk eventually gains Lt. Uhura's respect and trust as a result of the galactic emergency that gives all of them field commissions on starships, even though they aren't quite finished with their studies. Young Uhura is action Uhura; she does more than sit at a console.

The best part about this portrayal of Uhura is that everything she does is consistent with the older version of the character. As a fan of the series and, specifically, a fan of Uhura, I appreciate that in these new films we see the actual work of a communications officer. In the film *Star Trek*, we get a glimpse of the transmission scans that are a dull but necessary job when Christopher Pike, then-captain of the *Enterprise*, gives an order:

> *Pike*: Scan Vulcan space, look for any transmissions in Romulan.
> *Enterprise Communiations Officer:* Sir, I'm not sure I can distinguish the Romulan language from Vulcan.
> *Pike:* What about you? You speak Romulan, Cadet . . . ?
> *Uhura*: Uhura. All three dialects, sir.
> *Pike:* Uhura, relieve the lieutenant.
> *Uhura:* Yes, sir.

In a scene reminiscent of the original series episode about the discovery of the Son of God, Uhura discovers Romulan exchanges that endanger the galaxy and support Kirk's desire to go after a rescue mission. She boldly but respectfully conveys the evidence she has found:

> *Pike:* And you know of this Klingon attack how?
> [*Kirk glances at Uhura.*]
> *Uhura:* Sir, I intercepted and translated the message myself. Kirk's report is accurate.
> *Kirk:* We're warping into a trap, sir. The Romulans are waiting for us, I promise you that.
> [*Unsettled, Pike looks at Spock.*]
> *Spock:* The cadet's logic is sound. And Lieutenant Uhura is unmatched in xenolinguistics; we would be wise to accept her conclusion.

Uhura is also sent on missions that require her linguistic skills, and she holds her own in the combat scenes. In *Star Trek Into Darkness*, we see Uhura use her skills to engage enemy Klingons; she has a comprehensive understanding of honor as their way of life.

[*Uhura approaches the Klingon patrol, alone and unarmed.*]
Uhura: [*in Klingon*] I am here to help you. With respect,
there is a criminal hiding in these ruins. He has killed
many of our people.
Klingon: [*in Klingon*] Why should I care about a human
killing humans?
Uhura: [*in Klingon*] Because you care about honor. And
this man has none. You and your people are in danger.

Uhura is brave. She's bold. Her passion is channeled into
Starfleet because she believes in their mission: "To explore
strange new worlds, to seek out new life and new civili-
zations, to boldly go where no one has gone before." This
mission will take her away from her family and friends. It
will join her to a crew that will be her home for five years;
sometimes they will enter hostile areas, other times suffer
the loneliness of deep space. I admire her commitment to
disciplining herself, to understanding her role on the bridge
and in Starfleet as something greater than herself, and to
being constant and vigilant in the protection of the good.

ST. KATERI TEKAKWITHA

St. Kateri Tekakwitha suffered from isolation and exile.
Unlike the fictional Uhura, who joined Starfleet to explore,
St. Kateri's family imposed isolation upon her.

Tekakwitha was born in 1656 in the New York area of
the Mohawk River. She was the daughter of an Algonquin
Christian woman and a Mohawk man during a time when
both the Algonquin and the Mohawk tribes were a part of
the Iroquois nation at a time when there was violent unrest.
Trade disputes with the French and Dutch were common-
place. Tragically, a smallpox epidemic took the lives of her

parents and baby brother when Tekakwitha was just four years old. Although she survived the illness, it left her with scars, especially on her face.

Tekakwitha was adopted by an aunt and uncle, and she grew up to be a dutiful Mohawk woman. She was deeply moved by the Great Spirit, and by the time she was of an appropriate age to marry she had decided that she would rather dedicate herself to the Spirit. It caused some animosity within her family and community because her rejection of marriage was perceived to be a rejection of the community's values.

She withdrew, preferring to be alone and away from others rather than suffer from the disdain shown to her. At about this time, she became intrigued by the preaching of Jesuit missionaries who settled in the community.

Conflict and battles occurred constantly in the area surrounding their settlement, and Tekakwitha dedicated much of her time to tending the wounded. This brought her even closer to the missionaries, who also cared for the wounded, and over time she developed a deep yearning to learn more of Jesus Christ. This displeased her uncle, who wanted to limit the influence of Catholic missionaries.

When Tekakwitha was about eighteen years old, she approached a Jesuit priest, Fr. Jacques de Lamberville, to convert to Christianity. The following year she was baptized at Easter, scandalizing her family and the Mohawk community. She took the name Catherine, after St. Catherine of Siena—and became known as Kateri, the Mohawk translation. Today we call her by her baptismal name along with her birth name, Kateri Tekakwitha.

If life had been difficult for her before, now it was nearly impossible. She was accused of witchcraft and sorcery and was further isolated.

Within the year, Kateri relocated to Kahnawake, a Jesuit mission south of Montreal. The Jesuits had built the settlement for Native American converts, and it turned out to be a blessing for Kateri.

Orphaned as a young child, then shunned for her religious conversion, and now living away from her home in a northern territory, Kateri persisted in her faith, despite the isolation and loneliness she must have felt. She found a kinship with other young women in this new community, and her new faith flourished as she was able to dedicate herself to study and the Eucharist. She now lived with other Native Americans who shared not only a common culture but also a common faith.

The matron of the residence was a friend of her mother's, and Kateri settled in with her and with her older sister and brother-in-law, who had fled years earlier after converting to Catholicism. She also made a new friend, Marie-Therese, with whom she developed a beautiful spiritual friendship. This proved to be an uplifting experience for her. Finally, in spite of the distance and isolation from what she had known in her home village, Kateri found peace. Together with Marie-Therese, she influenced other young women in Christian practice—so much so that the women desired to found a community of young disciples. The formal group was discouraged by the priests, but Kateri continued to be a source of influence until she died a few years later at the age of twenty-four.

St. Kateri's influence continues today in my life. I feel drawn to her in a special way. St. Kateri's commitment to her faith, especially her desire to know Jesus Christ more intimately, speaks to me. Her wisdom in seeking spiritual friendships for encouragement as well as for companionship inspires me to continue to seek the same in my life. I have sometimes felt the sting of loneliness and isolation that comes from being different from the group.

Although I was much too young to remember political and religious persecution in Cuba, my life in the "northern territory" of the United States took me away from the warmth and sense of belonging that extended family offers. I grew up with only my immediate family, and with sporadic visits from grandparents and an aunt and uncle.

I imagine that Kateri thrived in her new surroundings as her relationships grew. Free to practice her faith, she found others with the same love of the Lord, and developed spiritual friendships with the women in her new home. This especially resonates with me. My family has always been an influential element in my faith formation, but I rarely experienced the joy and camaraderie of spiritual friends. I had plenty of friends who shared common interests, but a common love of the Lord was absent for a long time. St. Kateri reminds me of this fulfilling element of friendship and encourages me to continue to foster this kind of relationship.

St. Kateri's discerning spirit, which allowed her to bear patiently the pain of being shunned and to choose a life of quiet sacrifice instead of lashing out in anger, models the virtue of temperance I'd like to emulate.

WOMEN OF VIRTUE

Both women, the fictional Lt. Nyota Uhura and the canonized St. Kateri Tekakwitha, lived with an undercurrent of loneliness, cut off from their loved ones and having to make a life in a new frontier. Uhura and Kateri pursued the good—their desire to serve, in the first instance, the ideals of the Federation or, in the second, God was a good and worthy pursuit. These women not only had the desire for the good but also worked toward it with the disposition to sacrifice their immediate desires for the positive end.

In Nyota Uhura, we see a leader who demonstrates self-control and acts in accordance with reason. As a Starfleet officer, Lt. Uhura has practiced discipline throughout her training and career. Early in her career, Uhura struggled with self-control. She's a bit of a hothead, who speaks her mind openly and sometimes with abandon. She learns to temper this passion and enjoys a long and successful career in Starfleet, due in large part to her discipline and control.

Kateri Tekakwitha also demonstrates self-control, the cardinal virtue temperance, but she didn't always have it. When her family pressured her to marry and arranged a formal meeting with a suitor, Kateri jumped up from the meal where she was expected to serve the young man and ran away! She had to mature and practice this virtue until she was able to perfect it, not through of her human strength but through the gift of grace from God. She bore abuse from her family and her community for her refusal to marry. Her conversion to Christianity led to more persecution, which she handled with patience, without running away wildly or resisting her position in the community, until she was able to move to the Catholic mission.

The disposition to do good, and the discipline to guide these actions with restraint when emotions could easily take over reveal Nyota Uhura and Kateri Tekakwitha to be formidable models for this human virtue. Lt. Uhura seeks the good in the universe. St. Kateri seeks God. We see temperance in action through our fictional heroine, but through St. Kateri's life, we see how God gives us the grace to perfect this virtue in our lives and prepares us for relationship with the Divine.

PUTTING TEMPERANCE INTO ACTION

I must remind you here of an important truth: the Christian conception of life demands of all—whether highborn or lowly—a spirit of moderation and sacrifice. That is what God calls us to by his grace.

> There is, alas, a spirit of hedonism abroad today which beguiles men into thinking that life is nothing more than the quest for pleasure and the satisfaction of human passions. This attitude is disastrous. Its evil effects on soul and body are undeniable. Even on the natural level temperance and simplicity of life are the dictates of sound policy. On the supernatural level, the Gospels and the whole ascetic tradition of the Church require a sense of mortification and penance which assures the rule of the spirit over the flesh, and offers an efficacious means of expiating the punishment due to sin, from which no one, except Jesus Christ and His Immaculate Mother, is exempt.
>
> —St. John XXIII, *Mater et Magistra*

1. Think about an area in your life in which you are intemperate, in which you need to exercise discipline or self-control. Take this need to prayer. Ask the Holy Spirit to come to your aid. Then, begin to create a new habit with confidence! Keep at it, even if you don't get it right for some time.

2. The sacrament of Reconciliation is a good place to start as you work to create a habit of temperance. Check the schedule at a nearby church and go with an open heart. You can

also call and make an appointment with a priest. Like any-thing else, make a habit of going to confession.

3. Reexamine the role fasting plays in your life. Most of us are familiar with the traditional Catholic practice of fasting. Besides its penitential value, fasting teaches us that we *can* practice temperance in our lives. Consider other areas in your life where you can fast. Our dependence on technology, and sometimes over-indulgence in our phones and tablets, can lead to isolation and impersonal interactions. Fasting from the allure of the screen over the weekend, or during periods of the day, can remind us that these are tools, not extensions of ourselves.

CONCLUSION: THE QUEST FOR GOOD LEADS TO GOD

THE BLESSED VIRGIN MARY, OUR LADY OF GUADALUPE

Let not your heart be disturbed. . . . Am I not here, who is your Mother? Are you not under my protection? Am I not your health? Are you not happily within my fold? What else do you wish? Do not grieve nor be disturbed by anything.

—Our Lady of Guadalupe to
Juan Diego[1]

The fictional women in these stories, comic books, and television and movie productions seek the good as part of their character development. Their stories become playgrounds for us as we live vicariously through their adventures. They become real as we delve into the drama and allow our suspension of disbelief to take over and send us flying through the air, bending space and time to seek new worlds as they and we become heroes of rebellions on earth or in galaxies far, far away. That's the beauty of literature, that through our

149

imaginations we can explore the importance of justice and test the limits of our fortitude as well as practice prudence and temperance. These stories entertain us, but the characters can also easily become our heroes, models of virtues we'd like to emulate.

I wanted so much to be like Lt. Uhura, to interpret alien cultures for the command team on the *Enterprise*. I saw her strength and dignity, and knew it was something worth practicing in my life. I admired Agent Dana Scully, who calmly and methodically looked for solutions to the mysteries she encountered. I knew I could apply reason to finding trends and answers to the challenges I faced at work. I looked to Wonder Woman and found the motivation to work for justice not just in my personal life but in the community.

These characters, and the others in this book, inspire me. Through them, I imagined myself acting in ways that pushed my limits. I've said, on occasion, that some of these characters became role models for me.

If we're talking about isolating some of their characteristics, I'd say it's a good idea. There's nothing wrong with saying "I want to be strong," or striving to use reason before acting. Thinking about these virtues is a good place to start, and finding models, albeit fictional, can sometimes show us what these virtues look like in practice.

But this is only a place to begin.

If we can find inspiration in fictional characters whose lives are crafted by the writer's pen, how much more practical, more edifying is it to look to real holy women for inspiration? How much more consoling to discover a flesh-and-blood woman who experienced trials similar to mine and can demonstrate perseverance or fortitude in a setting that won't resolve itself after the next commercial or the carefully crafted cliff-hanger?

Real life needs real role models. The saints introduced in this book appeal to me because I can count on their having experienced life in all its sorrows and joys. Lives that, unlike fictional characters', are unscripted. We might think our era is the most difficult, but in truth, human beings have struggled with the same things for centuries: power, love, loneliness, anger, fear, disappointment, joy. To experience these things is to be human.

Whether we are drawn to the fictional heroines or the extraordinary saints, we can find something that resonates in us. We are daughters, sisters, wives, and mothers. We are friends, mentors, followers, and leaders. We are strong, vulnerable, wise, and noble. Some of us are all of these things. All of us are some of these things.

The fictional heroines aspire to a better world, and they work toward that end in larger-than-life ways because their context, their setting, is larger-than-life, be it on the page or on the cinematic screen. The saints, however, work for the common good away from the lights and cameras. Their scale might seem small, but it is led by the light of Christ. Often the small work of these holy women, when directed toward Christ, yields fruit for generations and generations. We see that in the lasting legacy of the Grey Nuns, in the work of the Sisters of St. Joseph, in the monasteries and cathedrals of Bavaria in Germany, and in the inspiration for prayerful lives, to name just a few.

DEVELOPING HEROIC VIRTUE

When we look to the saints, we are inspired to want to attain a habit of good conduct. As ordinary women, we cannot do this alone without God's grace. Nevertheless, we are called to live lives of holiness. We need to assume responsibility for our actions even as we receive help from God. Thus, to live a life of holiness is heroic. We are all called to be Christian heroes in our time. This idea astonishes us because we are so conditioned to think of heroes as larger-than-life personalities accomplishing dramatic deeds. We appreciate the grand gestures, but what we don't always realize is that to accept God's will and conform to it is a heroic act. That acceptance and conforming—that interior habit of striving to avoid sin, imperfections, and the concupiscence of our default failings—is heroic not because of some spectacular visible display, but because it requires spectacular humility: we fail, we seek forgiveness, we try again and again to get it right. This is Christian heroism.

Note the quiet virtue of the saints:

* St. Katharine Drexel quietly used her wealth to benefit generations of Native Americans and African Americans.
* St. Clare of Assisi put her trust in Jesus Christ in the Blessed Sacrament and saved her sisters, and the town of Assisi, from a Saracen invasion.
* St. Mary Magdalene loved Jesus, stayed faithful, and told the world of his Resurrection.
* St. Teresa Benedicta of the Cross went to her death in Auschwitz with dignity, offering up her suffering for the Jewish people.
* St. Cunegunde worked closely with her husband, the Holy Roman Emperor, to provide funds for churches and monasteries that still stand hundreds of years later, and she lived the last twenty years of her life in prayerful retreat in a monastery.
* St. Marguerite d'Youville suffered humiliation while building a health network that is lauded today in Canada.

★   St. Mary MacKillop endured the pain of excommunica-
    tion and a lifetime of defending her order while changing
    the face of Catholic education in Australia.
★   St. Kateri Tekakwitha bore wrongs patiently and lived
    in a foreign land for her love of Jesus and desire to serve
    him.

Some of these saintly women interested me because they
did unusual things. Of all the saints who, as role models,
offered me paths to holiness, these particular holy women
jumped off the pages to befriend me. These are saints I
admire, saints I respect, saints I want to emulate, and saints
I want to hang out with at the after-party.

In addition to being wonderful role models for us, the
saints are also powerful intercessors—prayer partners—for
us. Some of us are not shy about asking our friends to pray
for us. As we get to know more saints and discover their
qualities and find out to whom we are especially drawn, it's
good to call upon them, as our friends, for prayers.

THE BLESSED VIRGIN MARY

Mary, the Blessed Virgin and Mother of God, is the greatest
of all the saints. When we seek saints to emulate, to show
us the best way to become holy, Mary immediately comes
to mind as the perfect model of humanity. She is our spiritual mother, already loving us, nurturing us, and giving us
hope. Mary will always lead us to her son, Jesus Christ. St.
John Paul II, who had a very deep devotion to the Blessed
Virgin Mary, explains why Mary will, indeed, show us how
to love her son, Our Lord: "Christ is the supreme Teacher,
the revealer and the one revealed. It is not just a question
of learning what he taught but of 'learning him.' In this

regard could we have any better teacher than Mary? From the divine standpoint, the Spirit is the interior teacher who leads us to the full truth of Christ (cf. Jn 14:26; 15:26; 16:13). But among creatures no one knows Christ better than Mary; no one can introduce us to a profound knowledge of his mystery better than his Mother."[2]

I didn't always understand this, even though both cultural perspective and family practice consistently taught that the Virgin Mary as spiritual mother and saintly friend was always present. My mother often called on her protection and prayers for our family. Nevertheless, I thought of Mary in isolation, separate from her relation with God. There were two images I frequently associated with her: holding the child Jesus in the manger and resplendent in gold under the title of Our Lady of Charity. The first image I owe to years of Christmas cards with pictures of the Holy Family and a nativity set with loose pieces that allowed me to interact with that scene. I'd move all the other pieces around, but somehow even as a small child I never separated Mary from Baby Jesus. Never. That makes me smile now, that I knew even then that wherever Mary is, I will find Jesus.

The second image of Mary, Our Lady of Charity of El Cobre, is patroness of my birthplace, Cuba. Her presence, either in statues or pictures, was a reminder of our close ties to Cuba. It was only after I started school that I learned there are many, many, many titles of the Blessed Virgin Mary, and that like my beloved Our Lady of Charity, each of these titles carry some special meaning in its patronage.

When I started elementary school, I came to recognize Our Lady of Grace, with her beautiful blue mantle and open arms beckoning me to come close. I always looked forward to the May crowning! Our Lady of Lourdes was also a favorite and easy to identify with the flowing blue sash around her waist.

Statues and images of Our Lady of Guadalupe seemed to be everywhere. The more I saw this image, the more I became confused by the numerous symbols—she was filled with layers of meaning, and, because I didn't understand them, I dismissed the devotion. I had no idea of the magnitude of Mary's influence as Our Lady of Guadalupe. Years of tepid faith in young adulthood made it easy for me to dismiss her. My return to the faith, an ongoing discovery of the Lord and his merciful love, is a rediscovery of lost things, and it has included in recent years a reintroduction to Our Lady of Guadalupe.

After compiling my list of literary heroines for this book and looking to their dramatic adventures in interstellar travel and superhuman powers, I looked at the saints and wondered who could top this in scope and impact. I kept finding Our Lady of Guadalupe. I was sure there was inspiration there.

The apparition of Our Lady at Tepeyac Hill on December 9, 1531, came at a dark time in world history. The Protestant Reformation was gaining traction in Europe. Henry VIII of England would soon leave the Catholic Church and declare himself the head of the Church of England. The Ottoman Empire was close to defeating the Christian world. Catholic Christianity was at a crisis.

By 1521, the Spanish began colonizing what we now know as Mexico. They brought with them Franciscan, Dominican, and Augustinian monks to aid in the evangelization of the indigenous populations of the land. The Spanish discovered a powerful and advanced civilization in the Aztecs but were horrified by the practice of human sacrifice, which took thousands upon thousands of human lives in

tribute and appeasement to pagan gods. The Spaniards felt
a great sense of urgency in their evangelization efforts. They
estimated that 10 million souls were subject to the Aztec
rule, with 20,000 sacrificial murders of men, women, and
children per year. At the height of the sacrifices, 80,000 men
were killed over the course of four days.[3]

The Spaniards felt the only thing that would put an end
to this pagan practice was conversion. The Spaniards prayed
for God's intervention: they needed a miracle.

The morning of December 9, the Blessed Virgin Mary
appeared to Juan Diego, a poor but faithful servant of the
Lord who had the custom of attending daily Mass. When he
passed Tepeyac Hill on his journey, Juan Diego heard lovely
birdsong and a sweet voice calling to him. He followed the
voice and came upon the most beautiful vision of a lady.
She identified herself as the Mother of God and entrusted
Juan Diego with an errand. He was to go to the bishop and
recount everything he heard and saw, with the request that a
church be built on the spot where he had received the vision.
The Blessed Virgin assured him of the graces to accomplish
this task.

Juan Diego went directly to the bishop, Juan de Zumarraga, and told him everything. The bishop thanked Juan and
dismissed him, unaffected by the story. Disappointed, Juan
returned to the hill, where the Virgin Mary was waiting for
him. After explaining that his request went unheeded, Juan
humbly asked that the task be given to someone else, someone with more standing in the community so the bishop
would believe the request.

To this, the Blessed Virgin urged Juan to go back and
invoke her name. The next day, Juan went to the bishop, who
still didn't believe him, but this time Zumarraga requested
a sign. When Juan related this to the Blessed Virgin, she

thanked him for his perseverance and instructed Juan to return the next day for the sign.

Unfortunately, Juan Diego's uncle, Juan Bernardino, fell gravely ill overnight. The next morning, instead of returning to the Blessed Virgin for the promised sign, Juan bypassed the spot to summon a priest for his dying uncle. She appeared to him on the road, asking why he broke their appointment. Juan Diego replied that his uncle was dying and needed a priest, but he promised he would keep his word when he was done with the errand. The Blessed Virgin assured him of his uncle's good health, then she instructed Juan Diego to go to the top of the hill and gather an assortment of flowers. Juan Diego obeyed and returned with roses in his cloak that could not have grown in winter in the rough ground among so many weeds. The Blessed Virgin told Juan Diego to take the flowers to the bishop as a sign. When Juan Diego opened his cloak for the bishop, the image of the Blessed Virgin Mary appeared on the cloth. Bishop Zumarraga fell to his knees, immediately sorrowful for not believing Juan Diego.

The bishop built the church and placed the image on the tilma there for all to see. By 1539, only eight years later, almost nine million souls had converted to Christianity. The scope of that astonishing number is recognized as nothing short of miraculous. Or heroic. Juan Diego didn't have super powers. Instead, he humbly clung to his faith and his obedience to God's will.

LOVE IS ALL

The heroines in this book use their human virtues to fight against fictional wrongs. The saints demonstrate how virtue, when practiced in order to seek the Good, which is to seek God, aligns them with God.

The greatest model of virtue, the Blessed Virgin Mary,
Mother of God and patroness of humanity, continues to be
a loving mother to us, as she was to St. Juan Diego. As Pope
Francis tells us, we learn from Our Mother that "the only
power capable of conquering the hearts of men and women
is the tenderness of God. That which delights and attracts,
that which humbles and overcomes, that which opens and
unleashes, is not the power of instruments or the force of law,
but rather the omnipotent weakness of divine love, which
is the irresistible force of its gentleness and the irrevocable
pledge of its mercy."[4]

There are no super powers. No magic wands. No need
for capes. There is love.

BECOMING VIRTUOUS
HEROES AND HEROIC SAINTS!

The great danger in today's world, pervaded as it is
by consumerism, is the desolation and anguish born
of a complacent yet covetous heart, the feverish pursuit of frivolous pleasures, and a blunted conscience.
Whenever our interior life becomes caught up in its
own interests and concerns, there is no longer room
for others, no place for the poor. God's voice is no
longer heard, the quiet joy of his love is no longer felt,
and the desire to do good fades. This is a very real
danger for believers too. Many fall prey to it, and end
up resentful, angry and listless. That is no way to live
a dignified and fulfilled life; it is not God's will for us,
nor is it the life in the Spirit which has its source in the
heart of the risen Christ.

> I invite all Christians, everywhere, at this very moment, to a renewed personal encounter with Jesus Christ, or at least an openness to letting him encounter them; I ask all of you to do this unfailingly each day. No one should think that this invitation is not meant for him or her, since "no one is excluded from the joy brought by the Lord." The Lord does not disappoint those who take this risk; whenever we take a step towards Jesus, we come to realize that he is already there, waiting for us with open arms.
>
> —Pope Francis, *Evangelii Gaudium*

In this book I have shared some of the heroines that entertain me and saints that inspire me to seek a virtuous life, to seek the good. To seek God! Here are some final thoughts to ponder as you endeavor to do the same:

1. The fictional heroines in this book are fighting big injustices in their worlds: alien invasions, rampant crime, and manifestations of evil, to name a few. What are the injustices you see in your community? Can you identify local organizations that are working to address these concerns? Have you ever considered volunteering with these organizations?

2. In the first paragraph above, Pope Francis is speaking in broad terms about the causes of desolation and anguish in our world. Identify specific ways this is manifested in your intimate circle of family and friends or the community. List them. Pray about them. We sometimes forget that prayer is a powerful action. Recite the Rosary. Learn about the Chaplet of the Divine Mercy if you are not already familiar with it. Adopt some other devotion that fits with your personality and needs.

3. The saints in this book respond to Christ's call to actively do good. We don't have to establish schools and hospitals or financially support large institutions in order to do good. In fact, we can start small, in our families or circle of friends and maybe later expand to others outside our circle. Think about things you can do, simple things, such as spending time with someone who is lonely or offering to run an errand. Ask what you can do for someone. Remember the saints' heroic virtue is sometimes not found in doing the huge, dramatic thing but rather in doing the tedious, unnoticed thing.

4. Pope Francis extends a beautiful invitation to be in relationship with Jesus. This can mean a lot of different things to us. How can you take "a step" toward Jesus? Is it in prayer? Going to Adoration? Going to the sacrament of Reconciliation regularly, even perhaps after many years? Jesus is waiting for us!

ACKNOWLEDGMENTS

I want to thank a few people without whom this book would still be an idea scribbled in the pages of a notebook many years ago. All the superheroes at Ave Maria Press who had a hand in this—I said *no capes*, but you guys can wear them proudly. A lot of work goes into creating a book—thanks to you all! Amber Elder, my editor, kept me focused. Two wonderful writers, mentors, and dear friends, Lisa Hendey and Pat Gohn, practically made me wreck my car along a country road in the Deep South with their enthusiasm for this project. Pat, especially, reads anything I pitch her way and finds the merit in it—thanks a bunch. I'm grateful for your advice, your encouragement, and your prayers. My usual crew of prayer partners and pals, especially Linda and Yuyi. Mom and Pop. My sister and her Avengers and my brother and his X-Men. My kids have been wonderful cheerleaders, too, and sources of all kinds of information about superheroes. Thanks Spider-Man, Batman, Loki's mom, and Thor's dad. I couldn't have made sense of it without you. And finally, and always, my Superman—I love you! I promise I'll make dinner from scratch.

NOTES

INTRODUCTION

1. Benedict XVI, "Apostolic Journey to Valencia: Vigil of prayer at the conclusion of the Fifth World Meeting of Families in the 'City of Arts and Sciences'" Address, July 8, 2006.

2. Pat Gohn, *Blessed, Beautiful, and Bodacious: Celebrating the Gift of Catholic Womanhood* (Notre Dame, IN: Ave Maria Press, 2013), 10.

3. Francis, *Lumen Fidei*, Encyclical, June 29, 2013, 35.

4. Robert Barron, *Seeds of the Word: Finding God in the Culture* (Skokie, IL: Word On Fire, 2015).

PART I: SEEKING JUSTICE

1. *The Catholic Encyclopedia*, s.v. "justice," accessed November 30, 2016, http://www.newadvent.org/cathen/08571c.htm.

1. CRUSADERS OF JUSTICE AND LEARNING

1. Marguerite Lamb, "Who Was Wonder Woman 1?" *Bostonia*, Fall 2001, https://web.archive.org/web/20071208045132/http://www.bu.edu/alumni/bostonia/2001/fall/wonderwoman.

2. Jill Lepore, *The Secret History of Wonder Woman* (New York: Alfred A. Knopf, 2014), 198.

3. Jill Lepore, "The Man Behind Wonder Woman Was Inspired By Both Suffragists and Centerfolds," interview by Terry Gross, *Fresh Air*, NPR, October 27, 2014, http://www.npr.org/2014/10/27/359078315/

the-man-behind-wonder-woman-was-inspired-by-both-suffragists-and-centerfolds.

4. Lepore, *Secret History of Wonder Woman*, 22.

5. John Paul II, *Mulieris Dignitatem*, Apostolic Letter, August 15, 1988.

6. Peter Finney, Jr., "The Legacy of Saint Katharine Drexel," Franciscan Media, September 1, 2016, https://www.franciscanmedia.org/the-legacy-of-saint-katherine-drexel.

7. Thomas J. Olmsted, "Overturning Racial Prejudice: Mother Katharine Drexel and the Sisters of the Blessed Sacrament," *The Catholic Sun*, March 23, 2015. http://www.catholicsun.org/2015/03/23/overturning-racial-prejudice-mother-katharine-drexel-and-the-sisters-of-the-blessed-sacrament.

8. Thomas J. Olmsted, "Overturning Racial Prejudice: Mother Katharine Drexel and the Sisters of the Blessed Sacrament," *The Catholic Sun*, March 23, 2015.

9. Anne M. Butler, *Across God's Frontiers: Catholic Sisters in the American West, 1850–1920* (Chapel Hill: The University of North Carolina Press, 2012), 237.

2. BEACONS OF STRENGTH AND LIGHT

1. "Finn Meets Rey," *Star Wars: The Force Awakens*, directed by J. J. Abrams (San Francisco: Lucasfilm, Ltd., 2015), DVD.

2. "Now It Calls to You," *Star Wars: The Force Awakens*, directed by J. J. Abrams (San Francisco: Lucasfilm, Ltd., 2015), DVD.

3. "Luke Is Found," *Star Wars: The Force Awakens*, directed by J. J. Abrams (San Francisco: Lucasfilm, Ltd., 2015), DVD.

4. The Servants of the Pierced Hearts of Jesus and Mary, "St. Clare of Assisi," accessed November 30, 2016, http://www.piercedhearts.org/theology_heart/life_saints/clare_assisi.htm.

5. Benedict XVI, General Audience, September 15, 2010, https://w2.vatican.va/content/benedict-xvi/en/audiences/2010/documents/hf_ben-xvi_aud_20100915.html.

6. "Franciscan Friars T.O.R., "Canonization of St Clare of Assisi," accessed November 30, 2016, http://www.franciscantradition.org/clare-of-assisi-early-documents/78-the-acts-of-the-process-of-canonization-1253.

PART II: SEEKING PRUDENCE

1. *The Catholic Encyclopedia*, s.v. "prudence," accessed November 30, 2016, http://www.newadvent.org/cathen/12517b.htm.

3. IMPARTERS OF MERCY AND SERVICE

1. "Red in My Ledger," *The Avengers*, directed by Joss Whedon (Manhattan Beach, FL: Marvel Studios, 2012), DVD.

2. Ibid.

3. "The Safe House," *The Avengers*, directed by Joss Whedon (Manhattan Beach, FL: Marvel Studios, 2012), DVD.

4. "Avengers House Party," Avengers: Age of Ultron, directed by Joss Whedon (Manhattan Beach, FL: Marvel Studios, 2015), DVD.

5. Susan Haskins, *Mary Magdalen: Myth and Metaphor* (New York: Riverhead Books, 1995), 193.

6. Benedict XVI, *Urbi et Orbi*, Easter 2012, https://w2.vatican.va/content/benedict-xvi/en/messages/urbi/documents/hf_ben-xvi_mes_20120408_urbi-easter.pdf.

4. PARAGONS OF WISDOM AND TRUTH

1. John Shiban and Frank Spotnitz, "All Souls," *The X-Files*, season 5, episode 17, directed by Allen Coulter, aired April 26, 1998 (Los Angeles: 20th Century Fox Home Entertainment, 2009), DVD.

2. Kim Newton, "Revelations," *The X-Files*, season 3, episode 11, directed by David Nutter, aired December 15, 1995 (Los Angeles: 20th Century Fox Home Entertainment, 2009), DVD.

3. John Paul II, to George V. Coyne, Director of the Vatican Observatory, June 1, 1988, https://w2.vatican.va/content/john-paul-ii/en/letters/1988/documents/hf_jp-ii_let_19880601_padre-coyne.html.

4. Chris Carter, "Requiem," *The X-Files*, season 7, episode 22, directed by Kim Manners, aired May 21, 2000 (Los Angeles: 20th Century Fox Home Entertainment, 2009), DVD.

5. "Teresa Avila Quotes," the Official Website of The Carmelite Order, accessed November 30, 2016, http://ocarm.org/en/content/ocarm/teresa-avila-quotes.

6. Benedict XVI, Homily at the Mass for the Episcopal Ordination of Five New Bishops, September 12, 2009, https://w2.vatican.va/content/benedict-xvi/en/homilies/2009/documents/hf_ben-xvi_hom_20090912_ord-episcopale.html.

7. Augustine of Hippo, "Of the Morals of the Catholic Church," *New Advent: Church Fathers*, accessed November 30, 2016, http://www.newadvent.org/fathers/1401.htm.

8. "Teresa Avila Quotes," the Official Website of The Carmelite Order, accessed November 30, 2016, http://ocarm.org/en/content/ocarm/teresa-avila-quotes.

9. "Teresa Benedict of the Cross Edith Stein (1891–1942)," accessed November 30, 2016, http://www.vatican.va/news_services/liturgy/saints/ns_lit_doc_19981011_edith_stein_en.html.

10. John Paul II, *Fides et Ratio*, Encyclical, September 14, 1998, http://w2.vatican.va/content/john-paul-ii/en/encyclicals/documents/hf_jp-ii_enc_14091998_fides-et-ratio.html.

11. "Edith Stein Quotes," the Official Website of The Carmelite Order, accessed November 30, 2016, http://ocarm.org/en/content/ocarm/edith-stein-quotes.

12. "Teresa Benedict of the Cross Edith Stein (1891–1942)," accessed November 30, 2016, http://www.vatican.va/news_services/liturgy/saints/ns_lit_doc_19981011_edith_stein_en.html.

13. Ibid.

14. Ibid.

5. GUARDIANS OF DIGNITY AND CULTURE

1. Chris Claremont, *Uncanny X-Men #216*, April 1987.

2. "Women of Power—Storm," Comics Amino, accessed July 6, 2016, http://aminoapps.com/page/comics/7834442/women-of-power-storm.

3. "X-Men: Worlds Apart Vol 1–4," Marvel Database, accessed November 30, 2016, http://marvel.wikia.com/wiki/X-Men:_Worlds_Apart_Vol_1_4.

6. DEFENDERS OF FAIRNESS AND HONOR

1. J. K. Rowling, *Harry Potter and the Deathly Hallows* (New York: Arthur A. Levin Books, 2007).

2. J. K. Rowling, *Harry Potter and the Half-Blood Prince* (New York: Arthur A. Levin Books, 2005), 50.

3. Rowling, *Harry Potter and the Deathly Hallows*.

4. *Harry Potter and the Chamber of Secrets*, directed by Chris Columbus (U.K.: Warner Home Video, 2003), DVD.

5. Rowling, *Harry Potter and the Deathly Hallows*.

PART IV: SEEKING TEMPERANCE

1. *Merriam-Webster Online*, s.v. "temperance," accessed January 5, 2017, https://www.merriam-webster.com/dictionary/temperance.

7. CHAMPIONS OF CARING AND COMPASSION

1. William Modystack, *Mary MacKillop: A Woman Before Her Time*, (Chatswood, N.S.W.: New Holland Publishers, 2011), Kindle edition.

8. EXPLORERS OF PEACE AND FAITH

1. Nichelle Nichols, "Nichelle Nichols Answers Fan Questions Part 2," StarTrek.com, October 19, 2010, http://www.startrek.com/article/nichelle-nichols-answers-fan-questions-part-2.

2. Gene Roddenberry and Gene L. Coon, "Blood and Circuses," *Star Trek: The Original Series*, season 2, episode 25, directed by Ralph Senensky, aired March 15, 1968 (Los Angeles: Paramount, 2015), DVD.

3. Nichelle Nichols, "Nichelle Nichols Answers Fan Questions," StarTrek.com, October 18, 2010, http://www.startrek.com/article/nichelle-nichols-answers-fan-questions.

CONCLUSION

1. Jody Brant Smith, *The Image of Guadalupe*, rev. ed. (Macon, GA: Mercer University Press, 1994), 88.

2. John Paul II, *Rosarium Virginis Mariae*, Apostolic Letter, October 16, 2002, https://w2.vatican.va/content/john-paul-ii/en/apost_letters/2002/documents/hf_jp-ii_apl_20021016_rosarium-virginis-mariae.html.

3. "Our Lady of Guadalupe," EWTN website, accessed November 30, 2016, https://www.ewtn.com/saintsHoly/saints/O/ourladyofguadalupe.asp.

4. Francis, Apostolic Journey to Mexico: Meeting with the Bishops of Mexico gathered in the Cathedral, Mexico City, February 13, 2016, https://w2.vatican.va/content/francesco/en/speeches/2016/february/documents/papa-francesco_20160213_messico-vescovi.html.

MARIA MORERA JOHNSON is the author of *My Badass Book of Saints*, which won first place in the inspirational category at the 2016 Association of Catholic Publisher's awards. She also contributed to *The Catholic Mom's Prayer Companion* and *Word by Word: Slowing Down with the Hail Mary*. A *CatholicMom.com* blogger, Johnson retired in 2016 from her positions as a composition and literature professor and the director of English learning support at Georgia Piedmont Technical College.

Johnson has spoken at a number of events, retreats, and conferences, including the National Council of Catholic Women, Austin Women's Conference, and the Catholic Press Association. She also has been featured on CatholicTV and Busted Halo, and in *Catholic Digest* and *St. Anthony Messenger*.

Johnson is a native of Cuba. She and her husband, John, have three grown children and live in the Mobile, Alabama, area.

AVE

AVE MARIA PRESS

Founded in 1865, Ave Maria Press,
a ministry of the Congregation of
Holy Cross, is a Catholic publishing
company that serves the spiritual and
formative needs of the Church and its
schools, institutions, and ministers;
Christian individuals and families; and
others seeking spiritual nourishment.

For a complete listing of titles from

Ave Maria Press

Sorin Books

Forest of Peace

Christian Classics

visit www.avemariapress.com

AVE MARIA PRESS
Notre Dame, IN
A Ministry of the United States Province of Holy Cross